TWO WORLDS

BOOKS BY DAVID DAICHES

The Place of Meaning in Poetry
New Literary Values
Literature and Society
The Novel and the Modern World
Poetry and the Modern World
The King James Version of the English Bible
Virginia Woolf
Robert Louis Stevenson
A Study of Literature
Poems in English, 1530—1940 (editor)
Robert Burns
Willa Cather: A Critical Introduction
A Century of the Essay (editor)

TWO WORLDS

AN EDINBURGH JEWISH CHILDHOOD

DAVID DAICHES

Harcourt, Brace and Company

NEW YORK

first edition

Much of the material in Chapter 7 appeared originally in *The New Yorker* under the title "Trebblers, Bleggages, and Persians." Other parts appeared in different form as "My Father, and His Father" in *Commentary*.

LIBRARY OF CONGRESS CATALOG CARD NUMBER: 56-6656

PRINTED IN THE UNITED STATES OF AMERICA

286

To my Mother,
hoping that this new perspective on familiar
scenes will explain rather than disturb

CHAPTER 1

A windy spring day in Edinburgh, with bits of paper blown
down the street and two small boys from Sciennes School
kicking an empty tin can along the gutter. Across Melville
Drive, in the Meadows, workmen are busy building stands
and other wooden erections for the Highland Society's annual agricultural show, held in Edinburgh this year,
though generally further north. The year is 1919, and I am
six and a half years old. I am swinging on the heavy iron
gate of our house in Millerfield Place, an exercise which
gives me peculiar pleasure because we have only recently
moved into the house and this variety of gate, though common in the city, is new to me. I am wearing a pair of dirty
navy-blue shorts and a far from fresh brown jersey, and my
uncombed hair is blowing about my face. My mother
would be shocked indeed if she could see me now, but she
is ill in a nursing home in Davidson's Mains (it has the en-
chanting name of Silverknowe, and I imagine it as a shining castle set beside the sea) and the aunt who has come up
from London to look after my brother and sister and me
is out somewhere—with a young man, as my brother Lionel
and I knowingly tell each other, though this is mere sur-
mise: we are already precociously aware that my mother's

[7]

younger sisters should be looking for husbands. As for my
father, he is out at a meeting, or working in his study, or
busy trying to reconcile some dispute among different fac-
tions of his congregation. We children are free to join in
the rich street life of the Edinburgh keelies. The noise of
the wind and the rattle of the tin can sound like a tocsin of
freedom in my ears. There is an air of excitement in the
afternoon.

I hear my name called: "David! Where are you?" Lionel
is waving from the bottom of the street. "Come on and
watch the workmen," he calls. I hang on to the outside of
the gate as it swings round and clicks itself shut with the
automatic device that still fascinates me, then jump off and
run down to meet him. We cross Melville Drive, climb over
the iron railings that separate it from the Meadows (there
are several open entrances, but we prefer to climb) and
find ourselves amid heaps of stacked piles of wood. There
are several children swarming around these, and we join
them, clambering up and slipping down, chasing each
other between the stacks, shouting at the top of our voices.
Then one of the workmen, who are busy further down the
field, sees us and shouts: "Hey, get oot o' that!" We shout
louder than ever, and the workman makes a threatening
gesture. I find myself among a chorus of children chanting:
"Ha, ha, ha, ye canna catch me! Ha, ha, ha, ye canna catch
me!" I am not happy about this defiance of the workman,
but I am encouraged by being a member of a group, and
chant as loud as anyone. Then a shrill whistle blows, and
the cry goes up: "The parkie! The parkie!" and we all
stream off toward the Middle Meadow Walk as the park-
keeper, in his official uniform, whistles and waves at us.

Memory blurs the next part of the scene. Was that the
afternoon when we landed up in front of the little dairy in

[8]

Brougham Place and one of the girls went in and bought a ha'penny stick of barley sugar which she licked meanly and aggressively in front of our jealous eyes ignoring pleas to give everyone a "sook"? Or did we go in the other direction, past the tennis courts through the narrow ways that led into George Square and then—but one might go anywhere from there. How well we got to know certain corners of the city! All the streets that bounded the Meadows, of course: the austere flats of Marchmont, the sadly fading gentility of Buccleuch Place, the unpretentious little shops of Lauriston, where the cable cars bumped and clattered their way to Tollcross. And sometimes the more ambitious expeditions to Arthur's Seat, to find tadpoles and sticklebacks in Dunsappie Loch, or southward through the quiet shaded streets with their genteel detached houses and walled gardens to Blackford Hill, where uniformed nurses walked their gaitered brats and lovers lay behind the whin bushes. We walked, skipped, and ran unnoticed distances, often discovering with wonder that we were miles from home and returning breathless to be scolded for being so late and to murmur apologetically that we "didn't know the time."

1919 was the timeless year. The dislocation in family life produced by my mother's going to a nursing home, the sense of loss and bewilderment that Lionel and I both felt when we found the normal domestic routine shattered with the departure of the presiding genius of the home, gave way, under the influence of the natural resilience of childhood, to an abandoned exploration of our new freedom. Small as I was, my mother's illness gave me the freedom of the Edinburgh streets, through which I wandered, sometimes alone, often with Lionel, sometimes with a group of keelies, utterly insensible of the passing hours. Even on

[9]

school days I kept this indifference to time. I would dawdle on the way to school, stopping to play with a cat or throw stones for a dog, and find to my astonishment that I was late on arrival. On one occasion, I got absorbed in rattling a stick along the railings in a certain rhythm, and followed the streets wherever I could find railings. The thing was never to allow the rhythm to stop for a moment; when there were unavoidable gaps I had to tap the rhythm out on the pavement, stooping, or on a wall if there was one handy. I finally got to school at 10 o'clock—an hour late— and I still remember my bewildered sense of unreality when I found myself walking into a classroom long settled down to its day's work. The teacher was more puzzled than angry, and I was not punished. The incident sticks in my memory as a symbol of a state of mind which I associate entirely and uniquely with that spring of 1919: the pattern of the world I lived in had temporarily disappeared, routine was succeeded by a feeling of perpetual adventure, and I would discover with amazement that school began at the same hour every morning and that some strange thing the teacher made us do on, say, a Thursday afternoon was really the regular procedure for that day.

We did not go away for our summer holidays that year, because the whole family situation was in a state of confusion. So we stayed at home, and I wandered about the streets and played in the Meadows, absorbing the sights and sounds of an Edinburgh summer, so that the Edinburgh of 1919 is still in some ways more vivid to me than the city as it became later. Of course, the city has not essentially changed—it has changed less, I think, than almost any city in Britain—but the rattling cable cars were soon to be replaced by electric trams (which are now, in their turn, giving way to buses), the lamplighter, celebrated by Robert

Louis Stevenson, would in a few years be supplanted by an automatic device, and the feel of the city, which in 1919 was still, I think, essentially pre-World War I, was to undergo some subtle changes. But the lamplighter, whom I was to watch with such satisfaction in the early dusk of November and December, I never saw that summer: daylight stretched endlessly into the night, it seemed to me, and even in bed I could hear through my open window the cries of older boys playing cricket in the Meadows and the thud of bat against ball.

A year without time—yet it was only the secular year that lacked this dimension. There was another world, the world of orthodox Jewish ritual, which also claimed me. If I saw little of my father during the day—I would catch a glimpse of him walking down the street in his black coat and silk hat as I was playing cricket, using a schoolbook for a bat and three chalk lines on the wall for wickets—on Friday nights and Saturdays he presided over our world, and there was no shabbiness then, and no running around with keelies, and no forgetting of time. Somehow we always managed to be in our best clothes, with our faces washed and our hair slicked down with water, when my father came back from shul (synagogue) on a Friday evening (the service was standardized at several hours before sunset during the summer months, though the legal beginning of the Sabbath did not have to be until sunset); and round the candlelit table, Lionel and I wearing little green skullcaps and my father his accustomed black one, we talked in a politer accent than the one we employed in the streets, and discussed quite other matters. And as we sang the familiar *shir ha-ma'aloth* at the beginning of the postprandial grace, to the plangent minor melody that my father had learned from his father, the Meadows and Marchmont and Arthur's

Seat and Blackford Hill were forgotten and we were back in a world which stretched unbroken back through the Middle Ages to ancient Palestine.

But were they really forgotten? The two worlds, in my childhood, were not really separate. The synagogue in Graham Street, to which we walked across the Meadows every Saturday morning, was as much a part of the Edinburgh scene to me as the Royal Infirmary nearby, just as my father, rabbi of the Edinburgh Hebrew Congregation and virtual though not nominal head of Scottish Jewry, was a part of the religious life of Scotland. Indeed, one of my father's great aims in life was to bring the two worlds—the Scottish and the Jewish—into intimate association, to demonstrate, by his way of life and that of his community, that orthodox Jewish communities could thrive in Scotland, true to their own traditions yet at the same time a respected part of the Scottish social and cultural scene. It never occurred to me as a child that this combination was odd or unattainable (still less that it was *comic,* as the idea of Scottish Jewry seems to be to so many of my American friends); I thought of it as part of the nature of things, a natural result of the golden age in which we lived, so utterly different from the dark days of persecution and martyrdom about which we heard a great deal but never in any contemporary context. At school I did not join in the hymns with which the day's proceedings opened (in the elementary school we did not have prayers in hall, as we were to do in the senior school, but sang an opening hymn in class), though I got to know them perfectly well—"Onward Christian Soldiers," "Once in Royal David's City," and many others. I knew, from my tenderest years, that the theology of these hymns was all wrong and that the Jewish religion was of course *right;* but it was one's duty to be tolerant, and one had a friendly pity for one's non-Jewish companions who actually believed in the divinity of Jesus and dirtied their stomachs with *treife* food. As for my teachers and schoolmates, they had the Presbyterian respect for the People of the Book and regarded me with interest and sometimes even with a touch of awe. I used to boast that I was descended from King David of the Bible (which was a family tradition) and this gave me considerable prestige. I once overheard one of my classmates saying to another: "If Daiches' father had his right, he would be King of the Jews." Anti-Semitism I never met with at this time, and knew of it only as a phenomenon of the unhappy days of old, about which I read in such Anglo-Jewish storybooks as *Apples and Honey*.

There were some things, of course, that one did not talk about to one's schoolfellows, because they would never have understood. And, while at home we never called Saturday "Saturday" but always *Shabbos* (the Hebrew for Sabbath in the Ashkenazi pronunciation used by most European Jews before the Sephardi pronunciation of the Palestinian Jews came to be associated with the Zionist movement and with modern Hebrew culture), I was always careful to say "Saturday" at school. Only once do I remember making a mistake in vocabulary, and that was because I did not know that the Hebrew word *yomtov* (festival) was not current English usage. I was taking off my coat in the school cloakroom and chatting to a redheaded boy named Cunningham. It was one of the intermediate days of Passover, when we could go to school though of course we still ate only *Pesachdick* food. Cunningham offered me a sweet—it was a red jujube, as I clearly recall, though the incident happened in 1920—and, momentarily forgetting that it was Passover and that I could not eat any food that had not been specially prepared under rabbinical auspices, I popped it into my mouth. A second after I had done so, I realized what I had done, and hastily spat it out on the floor. Cunningham watched in amazement, and I tried to explain: "It's a Jewish *yomtov,* when we can only eat unleavened bread and specially prepared food that hasn't been near anything leaven." It was the utterly bewildered look on Cunningham's face that first taught me that *yomtov* was not a regular English word.

This was an exceptional incident, which accounts for its having stuck so clearly in my memory. Normally I had no difficulty at all in living in two worlds at once; both seemed to be satisfactorily related to the physical environment of Edinburgh. The synagogue in Graham Street—it had once been some sort of a chapel and had been made over—was in a decayed but fascinating part of the city; behind it the old streets tumbled down into the Grassmarket and Johnstone Avenue and the southern, precipitous side of Edinburgh Castle, and the approach from the east was by a picturesque narrow lane known as the Vennel, flanked by part of the old city wall. Many years later, when I was a student at Edinburgh University, my father's efforts resulted in the building of a fine new synagogue in a less run-down part of the city, and, though like everyone else I hailed the new building with satisfaction, the move was for me a disturbing break with my childhood and coincided (whether by chance or not I am not sure) with a far-reaching revaluation on my part of the relation between the two elements in my background.

But in 1919 I was untroubled by any conflict of beliefs or loyalties. The streets and meadows and hills of Edinburgh represented the timeless world, while my religion, with its fixed times and seasons, its recurring sabbaths and feasts and fasts, each with its own synagogue and domestic

[14]

ritual, was a world strictly divided into temporal units. On Saturday nights we would watch until three stars appeared in the sky, and then we know that the sabbath was over—*shabbos* was "out," as we put it—and one could strike a match or play the piano or revert to any of the usual weekday activities, even if my father, holding a lighted torch of twisted tapers, had not yet formally announced the change with a blessing over a glass of warm milk and a sniff at the silver spice box whose comforting odor was supposed to console one for the departure of the Princess Sabbath. In summer, no matter how late we stayed up, we were in bed before the dividing line (one could bring *shabbos* in earlier than the legal time on Friday evening, but one could not send it out on Saturday night before the sun had completely set); in winter it came early, and in the short days of December and January there was a whole secular evening to follow, just as on the previous evening candles were lit and the curtains drawn and the world of Jewish time established the moment we got home from school.

In the long summer evenings, when the sabbath seemed to be stretching on forever, we would go for sedate walks through the more genteel streets to the south, carrying a sort of invisible wall with us as we moved through a working and playing world. It never occurred to me to resent this restriction on my freedom, to feel ill-used because I could not join the wild street play of the children who were often my casual playmates on other days of the week. But I preferred to avoid passing them, and to walk in the quieter ways where they were not likely to be. This was because I would be wearing my best clothes, and I disliked to be seen, when dressed up, by boys who were in their ordinary weekday attire. This matter of clothing was the only thing that I remember disturbing my relations with the non-Jewish world in my childhood, and this was especially so after my mother had come home from the nursing home (I think in the middle or late summer of 1919) and briskly undertook the improvement of our dress. I had no objection to wearing neater and cleaner school clothes, because they were the same kind of clothes that the other boys at school wore, but I did occasionally feel uncomfortable when, dressed in a dark suit on a Saturday or a festival, I passed some of my friends wearing open cricket shirts or jerseys and blazers.

The school I went to—George Watson's Boys' College, which took boys from infancy right up to university entrance—was on the northern side of the Meadows, and the senior boys would use the Meadows as their playground during the lunch interval. In the late 1920's, when I was in the senior school, I would have to walk through groups of playing classmates on my way home from shul on a Jewish festival, for the way to the synagogue from our house ran through the Meadows and by the school, and by some unhappy coincidence the service on Passover or Tabernacles or other of the festivals would conclude just as the lunch interval commenced. My brother and sister and I were, of course, always absent from school on these festivals, and that did not worry us particularly—at least, not until our last years at school, when we were preparing for important competitive examinations, and missing a lesson might be serious. The teachers and the pupils accepted the fact that the Daiches boys were liable to be absent at odd times for religious reasons, and often on my return after such an absence someone would ask: "Was it a fast or a feast?" That side of it was perfectly all right, and I would enjoy myself explaining to teachers or classmates just what the particular festival was and wherein lay its historic significance (I am

[16]

talking now of the time when I was fourteen or fifteen). Indeed, I remember several times explaining the difference between the Jewish and Christian religions to my classmates, especially to the son of the Prestonpans minister, with whom I went about a great deal in my last years at school; and I remember lending him, and several of the masters, my pocket edition of Paul Goodman's *History of the Jews,* which I used to carry around with me in order to be able to answer questions and cite facts and figures whenever challenged. But walking through a group of boisterously playing classmates when I was dressed up in my festival clothes I found uncomfortable, particularly since my mother, who had the highest ideals for her children both sartorially and in other respects, insisted that Lionel and I wear suits consisting of black jackets and waistcoats and long striped trousers—a garb unknown among Edinburgh boys, who at that time always wore shorts (and sometimes the kilt) until they were fully grown. This battle of the suits played an important part in my childhood. My mother, who was born and brought up in Liverpool, remembered how gentlemanly little English boys had looked, and with the best of intentions tried to model us on them. Lionel seemed rather to take to this mode of dress (to which, being in the legal profession, he still clings), but I found it embarrassing. In my secret heart I wanted to wear a kilt, but I knew that I had no hereditary right to one, and never breathed a word of my ambition to anybody.

It was in my teens, too, that I established myself in the Scripture class (taught, in the year I am thinking of, by a classics master) as an authority on the Hebrew text of the Bible, and when we were studying Old Testament history I would lay my Hebrew Bible conspicuously on the desk before me. "What does the Hebrew say, Daiches?" the teacher would ask when he came to some obscure incident, and sometimes after class the boys would crowd round and ask me for the true meaning of one of the franker sexual references. All this ministered to my pride; and I had been encouraged from my earliest years to be proud of my religion and also of my family background. Whether we were really descended from King David I do not know—the story went that my grandfather's sister lost the only complete copy of the family tree on a journey to Palestine—but I believe we can trace our descent from Rashi, the eleventh-century French Jewish Biblical scholar, and my more immediate paternal ancestry is thick with rabbinical scholars and Talmudists of considerable eminence. Looking back, I think now that family pride was more important to all of us than more general religious pride; from earliest childhood Lionel and I regarded ourselves as aristocrats. We constructed private myths about our aristocratic Jewish lineage, which gave us immense satisfaction. My mother has recently expressed surprise and doubt at my impression of the intense family pride that surrounded my childhood, but there is no doubt in my mind that both she and my father—consciously or unconsciously—managed at home to suggest that we were a very special family, and what might be considered good enough for other families (either Jewish or non-Jewish) was not necessarily good enough for us. We were proud of being Jewish, of course; but we were far prouder of being called Daiches.

You would have seen little of this pride, however, if you had watched us playing in the Edinburgh streets, for it was only at special moments that one recalled the importance of one's ancestry. Looking back, it seems to me that I must have largely depended on this family pride to compensate

[18]

me for the minor frustrations and irritations which, even in the most congenial atmosphere, cannot but play some part in the life of a Jewish boy in a gentile environment. As I grew older, I began to see important things that I was missing. That we could take no part in school games or sports—which were always on Saturdays—Lionel and I took completely for granted from the beginning, and since neither of us was particularly interested in formal games or athletics this did not bother us much. But when I entered the senior school I discovered that the school literary society met on Friday nights, and this was one activity where I would have shone. It was unthinkable, of course, that I could have attended—the sacredness of Friday night was absolutely unquestioned in our family—but I used to look wistfully at the notices announcing the meetings and allowed myself to wish at least that the meetings might have been held on another day of the week. My only school activities outside the classroom were playing the violin in the school orchestra and attending the meetings of the Field Club on Tuesday afternoons to listen to lectures, accompanied by magic-lantern slides, on anything from "Life in Pond and Stream" to "A Visit to Paris." Both of these activities came very low down in the schoolboy's heirarchy of values.

It was not as though I had Jewish friends to whom I could turn for real companionship. The Edinburgh Jewish community was small—about four hundred families—and there were very few Jewish boys at Watson's. Though I knew the other Jewish children in the city, and regularly attended their parties in the winter party season, I was intimate with none. In some respects I felt more cut off from them than from my Presbyterian classmates and street companions. My father, whose personality and scholarship had made him a public figure in Edinburgh, was known wherever he went: his formal bearing, his small brown beard (which diminished almost to nothing with the years), his dignified black clothes and increasingly solitary silk hat, were recognized everywhere, and people would whisper as he passed: "That's the Jewish rabbi," or even, "That's Dr. Daiches." ("Rabbi," incidentally, was often pronounced in Edinburgh as "rabbie," the familiar Scots form of "Robert," and occasionally my father received letters addressed to R. S.—or Robert S.—Daiches, Esq.) Among the Jewish community he was both loved and respected—almost feared at times, perhaps—and the prestige he had won throughout the city, and indeed throughout the country, increased their respect for him enormously. But the result of this was to divide Lionel and me from my Jewish contemporaries. We were the rabbi's sons; people must watch their step in front of us. This attitude reinforced the natural aloofness of the Daiches family, and the result was that I felt at least as strong a barrier dividing me from the Jewish boys of Edinburgh as from my Christian schoolfellows and playmates.

But the city had no barriers against me; the sights and sounds and smells of Edinburgh crowded in upon my senses day after day and year after year. To this day I cannot hear the whirr of a lawnmower without being taken back at once to a summer afternoon in Millerfield Place—how childhood memories seem to cluster around summer!—with Mr. Fyfe (his son is now Lord Chancellor) at the bottom of the street cutting the grass in his front garden and the shouts of boys coming up from the Meadows; nor can I see lilac or laburnum without remembering those quiet Edinburgh streets between Marchmont and Blackford Hill where the heavy blossomed trees leaned over the stone garden walls and the air was hung with a scented quietness and it seemed as though the sun stood still in the sky and time was arrested forever; nor see a horse-drawn cart without hearing again the rattle of early morning milk-traps or the heavy clatter of vans drawing cases of Leitch's lemonade or Dunbar's mineral waters or sacks of coal along the uneven paving of Melville Terrace. A chalk mark in the street brings back the girls playing "peevers" on the Edinburgh pavements, or skipping to their traditional chants, or counting out for some game in weird rhymes. And the traditional chanting of Hebrew prayers brings back the Meadows and Lauriston Place and the Vennel and the old synagogue in Graham Street (pulled down over twenty years ago) with its mixed congregation of Yidish-speaking immigrants and native-born Edinburgh Jews with their strong Edinburgh accent even in the singing of Hebrew hymns.

If in the summer I moved between the timeless world of outside play and a religous world of hebdomadal and seasonal ceremony, in the winter the two worlds shifted their relationship somewhat. In middle or late autumn the procession of the festivals started: Rosh Hashanah, New Year, first, then the crowning solemnity of Yom Kippur, the Day of Atonement, and finally the more relaxed Feast of Tabernacles. Thus the religious calendar asserted itself, after a summer with nothing but the weekly Sabbath, and with it the claims of the domestic hearth even more than those of the synagogue. The candlelit table, the family circle round the fire, my mother in her best dress, my father very much the contented family man after the solemnities of the synagogue—this was the Daiches family not only practicing its religion in the same way that its ancestors had done for centuries, but also reasserting its own integrity, preening itself, one might almost say, on being itself and not any other family. I don't say that we were wholly conscious of this, and I am sure that my father would have been horrified if anyone had described what was going on in this way, but looking back now I can see so clearly what an important part family pride played in these proceedings. Of course there was more to it than that. We all knew the importance that Judaism attached to family life and happy family observance, and our family was a perfect example of this in many respects; but for the Daiches family these occasions were also demonstrations of the family's self-sufficiency, confirmations of my childhood impression that the outside world, Jewish and Christian, existed as a background to our family, that other Jews were necessary for my father to to preach to and for him to help and lead, and non-Jews were there so that Jews should be known by their difference from them and so that my father could show how it was possible for the two worlds to be reconciled. I would look at my father sitting relaxed in his chair by the fire after dinner on a Sabbath or festival eve, and glow with a satisfaction that he was there and we were there and that everything was as it was.

Perhaps this is misleading. Have I given the impression that we enjoyed asserting ourselves as a family and cheered each other with a sense of our own importance? That would be quite wrong. It was all unconscious and effortless; we simply took it utterly for granted that we were an aristocratic family. That was something too obvious to mention. Our evenings by the fire after the Sabbath or festival dinner were informal and often humorous. Though Lionel and I went over the next day's "portion of the Law" in the traditional cantillation with our father, we also clowned fairly often, or engaged in mimicry (both of members of the Edinburgh Jewish community and of our own relations), while our parents smiled indulgently. Once, after the Seder service on Passover, I read to the family and guests a complete and elaborate parody of the Passover Haggadah, the order of service for the Seder; it never occurred to anyone that there was anything sacrilegious about it. Lionel and I from an early age set up as family entertainers (in my early teens I brought out singlehanded a monthly magazine called "The Family Entertainer") and there was often a species of cosy hilarity accompanying our Sabbath and festival evenings.

As the days grew shorter and Friday nights came earlier and lasted longer, the impression of the family as asserting its unity and, in a sense, its superiority at the end of the week, thereby setting a seal on the week's activities, would grow, and the city became an exciting background against which the cosiness of the domestic interior was highlighted. It was dark by four in midwinter, and coming home from school in the December dusk to tea in the dining room with the fire blazing and the red silk shade of the low-hanging chandelier lit up by the bulbs inside, one was conscious of a theatrical shift in the scene, as of a curtain lifted. And in the streets outside, the little fruit shops and fancy-goods stores and grocers, decorated for the Christmas season with mounds of tangerines set in half-globes of silver paper, with net stockings filled with cheap toys and bells of colored paper hanging in the window, would repeat the theme in a different key: festive windows lit in the darkness to challenge the December murk. On a clear day the dusk would turn true violet in color, and the dark outline of the Castle would stand out on the horizon in romantic gloom. (Many years later they took to floodlighting

[23]

it, which was picturesque but not the same thing: the gas light in the windows of the little shops in the back streets, with their tinsel decorations and cheap Christmas goods, was the most moving illumination I ever saw in Edinburgh.) We did not observe Christmas, of course; we kept, instead, the more or less contemporary Jewish festival of Chanukah; but the Christmas atmosphere always seemed proper and acceptable, and it never seemed to me that I was in any way cut off from it in virtue of our not keeping the actual day. And the colored Chanukah candles, and my father's tenor voice leading us in the old hymn of *maoz tsur,* "Rock of Ages," mingled in my mind with the illuminated windows, with the silver tangerines and the boxes of crackers and the loops of tinsel, with the old Castle looming black in the purple evening and the sense of the darkening city beyond falling away to the Firth of Forth. Chanukah was Edinburgh in December.

It was strange, I suppose—though it did not seem strange to me then—this easy blending of Christmas and Chanukah, of Jewish history and Edinburgh atmosphere. Chanukah, the Feast of Lights, commemorates a miracle wrought in the Temple after the successful revolt by Judas Maccabeus and his heroic companions against the paganizing forces of Antiochus Epiphanes: when I was fifteen I wrote an "epic poem" on the subject, modeled, in style and verse form, on Scott's *Marmion.* Yet Chanukah to us was also the distribution of "pokes" of sweets to Jewish children after the special service in the Graham Street synagogue, and walking home afterward in the dark December evening, savoring the atmosphere of Edinburgh at night during the Christmas season. There was, of course, much less commercial ballyhoo about Christmas then than there is now, and besides, Scotland, whose established

[24]

Presbyterian church had long minimized celebration of Christmas Day as "Popish," celebrated the season rather than the day. The real Scottish festival was Hogmanay, New Year's Eve, in which we could participate as a purely secular feast. Jewish New Year was a solemn occasion, the ushering in of the period of penitence which culminated in the Day of Atonement ten days later; the Scottish New Year was an utterly different sort of affair, and though we never celebrated it as a family, we were at liberty to identify ourselves with its celebration by others. I am not sure if I have set out all the factors in their proper logical emphasis. Perhaps there were other reasons for what, in retrospect, I can see as the effortless reconciliation of a very Jewish Chanukah feeling with a very Edinburgh feeling of celebration. I doubt if I would even have considered this worth commenting on if I had not been struck with the way in which Jewish parents get fussed about the Christmas problem today. It is a problem that I never remember once being bothered about in my childhood. (But no sooner have I written this than I ask myself whether it is wholly and absolutely true. I seem to remember a faint twinge— of regret? of simple envy?—when the red mail vans came up our street, delivering Christmas presents, and I knew they would not stop at our door.)

All this is the cumulative impression of many years, and takes me far beyond the year 1919, with which I began. It was in the beginning of 1919 that we moved to Edinburgh from Sunderland, where I was born, and that move was the true beginning of my life as I remember it; for I remember my childhood as a developing relation between family tradition and my sense of Edinburgh. Of course there were other important elements, too: there was school, for example, where so much of my weekday life was spent;

there were the fishing towns of Fife where, from 1920 on, we went for our annual summer holiday; there was my discovery of poetry and my conviction, formed about the age of thirteen, that I was destined to be a second Shakespeare. These elements have each their own significance, and perhaps in the final summing up some of them will be found to be the most significant of all. But, apart from a few fragmentary recollections of my Sunderland days, my remembered life begins in that timeless spring of 1919, when I romped through the Edinburgh streets with all my senses wide open and with no preconceptions as to what I should find; and in the background my father, writing in his study, setting out to attend a meeting or conduct a service, and at the week-end gathering his family together to remind it of its identity and its heritage and to fortify its pride.

CHAPTER 2

In Britain in the 1920's a family did not need to have much of an income in order to employ a maid, and though our family's financial position was always precarious we generally had one. It seemes to me that the later maids never had the character or personality of those we had in my earlier childhood. In my seventh year, and at intervals afterward, my brother and sister and I were left much with maids because of the illness of my mother, and the maid's character therefore mattered a great deal to us. The further back I go, the more satisfactory the maid seems to have been; she was more efficient, more interesting to us children, and stayed for a longer period instead of disappearing without notice after receiving her first month's pay as some of them were to do later.

I have a dim memory of a maid we had in Sunderland, called Kate Hoffman, whose German name caused her some embarrassment during World War I. But the first maid whom I remember clearly is Bella, who was not really our maid but the maid employed by a family with whom we stayed for some weeks on our first arrival in Edinburgh early in 1919. It was at this time that my mother (who had never fully recovered her strength or her spirits after bearing her third child in three years, though she was to make a full recovery later) suffered that "nervous breakdown," as it was then called, which necessitated her resting for some months at a nursing home, and Bella, robust, energetic, good-humored, and omniscient, was pretty much in charge of us. She left us to ourselves most of the time, but occasionally she would take us on odd and interesting excursions—for example, to watch the buses having their gas bags filled, for this was just after the World War and the petrol shortage had forced the buses of the Scottish Motor Traction Company to use instead of petrol some kind of gas (in the scientific, not the popular American, sense of the word) which was contained in large balloon-like bags that covered the bus roof. Years later I used sometimes to wonder whether I had not dreamed about those heavy S.M.T. buses threading the Edinburgh streets underneath their crazy gas bags; it seemed too fantastic to be true; but in 1944, in London, I saw a private car with a similar contraption, and my memory of 1919 was vindicated.

It seems to me, looking back now, that those excursions with Bella were often strange and abrupt. I remember finding myself more than once having tea with an unknown family in an unfamiliar house, whither I had been whisked off by Bella to be left there until she had time to call for me. I am not sure to this day who those families were, though they were probably friends of the people with whom we were staying, and I remember how my initial sense of bewilderment at being deposited among strange but kindly faces soon gave way to a pragmatic acceptance of each situation as I found it and a determination to eat as much as I could in an unobtrusive way. I associate these visits with seed cake, of which I ate large quantities on principle, as it were, without really liking it. Even now,

[28]

the taste of seed cake, like Proust's *madeleine,* brings back the smell and clatter of a crowded tea table in a flat in Leith Walk or Spottiswood with well-meaning but to me thoroughly offensive grown-up faces looming through piles of cakes and sandwiches to ask fatuous questions about my personal life. Once there was a young lady at a piano warbling a love song at an enraptured young man, and I delighted all the grown-ups present by saying sententiously (having recently seen or heard the remark somewhere): "People who write love poems should remember that the only word which rhymes with 'Cupid' is 'stupid.' " This earned for me a reputation for literary precocity which I cheerfully accepted. I needed all the helps I could to stand up to the strangeness of these tea parties which so suddenly materialized out of nowhere. It seemed to me that there were people who, like the Mad Hatter, the March Hare, and the Dormouse, were perpetually having tea, and that other people wandered in and out among the cups and saucers at will.

Soon after, we moved to our own house in Millerfield Place where, after my mother had come back from the nursing home, we had a procession of maids of our own. Training a Scottish maid to work in a rabbinical household was an elaborate business: my mother would have to explain about the different dishes for meat and milk, the impossibility of washing dishes in soap (which contained animal fat), the importance of using different dishcloths for *milchig* and *fleischig* dishes (blue bordered for the former, red for the latter), the special requirements for Sabbaths and festivals. They were always very astonished at first, but soon came to take it all as a matter of course, picking up the appropriate Hebrew or Yiddish terms and pronouncing them with a rich Scots accent. My mother always took

[29]

a great interest in the maids' personal life, lending them books to read, letting them have an extra afternoon off if there was anything especially interesting on in town, giving them help and advice in their love affairs and other problems. Often they came to us raw and untrained and my mother worked with them and trained them thoroughly in the various arts of household management. To us children a maid was a companion and a source of all kinds of odd information. (Not all of the information was accurate. For years I believed that lunatics were removed to the asylum in a yellow cab with red wheels, because a maid had told me that, as a joke I suppose.) They generally came from neighboring towns and villages—Bathgate in one case, I remember, and in another Bo'ness—and occasionally one of them took me to her home for tea, an experience looked forward to chiefly for the bus or train ride involved.

One of our most successful maids, who stayed with us for a long time and only left to get married, was a girl called Dorothy Greenwood, who hailed from Yorkshire. She had an extraordinary gift for storytelling, and would relate macabre tales of haunted castles which occasionally led to my waking screaming in the night. Many years later, when I read Horace Walpole's *Castle of Otranto*, I recognized the genre as that to which Dorothy's stories had belonged, though I am sure she had neither read nor heard of Horace Walpole. Other maids were less gifted. We once had an elderly maid called Jane, who had the fascinating habit of muttering to herself, though we could never make out what she said. One day Lionel and I got up very early and crept quietly downstairs to hide behind the dining-room sofa while Jane laid the breakfast, so that we could hear what she was saying to herself. But though we were successful in concealing ourselves and had the satisfaction of seeing her dust the room and set the table oblivious of our watching eyes, we were not able to make out a word of her mutterings. She was a pathetic old soul, and how she landed as a housemaid at her time of life I don't know.

Every year after World War I it grew increasingly difficult to get a good maid, at least for the wages that we could afford to pay. I remember especially how delinquent many of the later ones were at dusting. My mother would come downstairs and run her finger over the sideboard or the mantel, which was supposed to have been dusted that morning. She would then inspect her finger, find it covered with dust, and exclaim disgustedly: "Pig!" (But she never said this when the maid was present, being always gentle and courteous with them.) We children would make good-humored fun of her finger-testing, and to this day it is a joke among us to run a finger over a piece of furniture, examine the finger, and exclaim, "Pig!"

While my mother was well, my father had little contact with the maid. When he was not out at one of his innumerable meetings or at the synagogue he stayed in his study, reading or writing, and his study was a sacrosanct room which no maid entered, except when he was out. But the maid had the duty of answering the door, and ushering into the study people who called on my father, who would range from heavily bearded emissaries from rabbinical colleges in Eastern Europe to the Professor of Hebrew or of Logic and Metaphysics at Edinburgh University. Some of the callers knew no English, and curious, mutually unintelligible dialogues between maid and visitor would take place at the front door until my father came out to see what was going on or my mother came to the rescue. Sometimes an extremely impressive-looking visitor would turn out to be a crook: I remember a venerable-looking couple of gentlemen who claimed to be collecting for some European Yeshivah but whom we later discovered, with the help of the police, to have been collecting only for themselves. My father was continually being visited by collectors, beggars, *émigrés*, scholars, Talmudists, clergymen, distressed persons, eccentrics, and fakers, and he was generally able at a glance to distinguish the genuine from the counterfeit—something which I was never able to do, for I found myself nearly always most impressed by the least worthy.

I remember once two young men arrived at the house, speaking only Yiddish, and alleged that they had just arrived by cargo boat at Leith from some Baltic port, and were penniless and starving. My mother made them a huge meal, while my father cannily telephoned the appropriate officers at Leith to find out whether in fact a boat from the Baltic port had arrived that day. He found that none had. It turned out eventually that the men had arrived by train from Newcastle, and that they were making a systematic tour of the Jewish communities of Britain, telling a different hard-luck story at each one and collecting free meals and substantial sums in cash. Such gross abuses were, of course, infrequent; most of the distressed persons who arrived at our house in search of help were in genuine need; but the well-known charitableness of Jewish communities toward needy brethren from any part of the world did encourage the occasional confidence trick.

My mother had to be ready at a moment's notice to give any one of this miscellaneous collection of visitors a meal. She was not often caught unprepared, but I recall one Wednesday afternoon (early closing day, when the shops shut at one) when she was suddenly called upon to provide a substantial repast for a hungry *meshullach* (emissary from a Yeshivah, abroad) at the awkward hour of 3:30 P.M. The only food in the house was for the family's dinner that night. I was sent to borrow some eggs from a neighbor, and the *meshullach* had to be content with boiled eggs and vast quantities of bread and butter, which he ate, it seemed to me, with an almost contemptuous air. On another occasion my mother had just prepared supper for my father and herself and, by some chapter of accidents, had nothing in the way of food left in the house apart from what she had prepared, when a venerable-looking gentleman made his way unannounced into the dining room. My mother, in some embarrassment, explained the circumstances, and apologized for not being able to give him a meal, at which he smiled and sat down at her place and fell to. My mother went into the kitchen and shared the maid's supper.

To the maid, my father was always the "Master" or the "Doctor," and was referred to with a certain amount of awe. "We must have lunch prompt today," my mother would say, "because the Doctor has a meeting at two o'clock." The maid must have thought of my father as moving in a mysterious multilingual world, full of oddly dressed characters and strange and impressive rituals. After the main meal of the day we would say the long Hebrew grace, singing out the beginning and the end of certain paragraphs, and the maid would move around the table collecting the dirty dishes and listening. If my father introduced a new tune, as he would occasionally do, the maid might comment to one of us later in the kitchen: "Yon was a nice tune the Doctor had today." When we were very young we had no self-consciousness at all in discussing these matters with the maid; but as we grew older we became more reticent.

When my mother was ill, and she had a number of spells

of illness, sometimes fairly long, in the 1920's, my father would come into closer contact with the maid. He would have to go into the kitchen sometimes and give orders himself, speaking always in a tone of extreme politeness, and referring to my mother as the "Mistress." "Oh, Mary, the mistress would like you to bring up a cup of tea. Would you please do that?" "I think we might have dinner now, Mary." He was not exactly shy of the maid, but he clearly felt that this was a kind of human being of which he had no real knowledge and he spoke to her with a certain caution, as one might speak to an animal of whose disposition one was ignorant. There were sometimes quite long periods when there was no maid, and Mother was ill, and my father would wrestle with domestic affairs himself. There was one period when he used to get up early and make porridge while we children helped in various ways (I used to light the fires and clean the shoes), and I have a clear picture of him standing by the stove in his dressing gown, stirring the porridge while admonishing us to hurry or we would be late for school.

The most serious problem that arose when we had no maid was the lighting of fires and the turning on of the gas on the Sabbath, when such activity was forbidden. There was a little grocery shop, Cameron's, round the corner, where we used to get some of our groceries, and they had a messenger boy ("message boy" was the term we used) whom we were sometimes able to get to come in and put a match to the fire or the gas stove. The boy regarded us as quite mad. "See," he said to my mother the first time he was asked to come in and light the gas, "it's quite easy. Ye just turn this wee handle and then pit the light tae the wee holes." "I know how to do it," replied my mother calmly, "but this is the Jewish Sabbath and I may not strike a light." The

[34]

boy's jaw dropped, and he looked at her sideways, half scared. But later he came to take it all for granted. Sometimes, when Cameron's boy was not available, my mother would go into the street and ask anyone she could find to come in and light the gas. I remember an occasional bewildered stranger being led into the kitchen to put a match under the soup. When I was a little older I would ask my father what one was supposed to do in a community where everybody was Jewish and there were no goyim to light the gas, but I cannot remember ever receiving a satisfactory answer. The logical answer, I suppose, would have been that everybody would have to stay cold, and we had some experience of that state on winter Saturday afternoons when there was no maid and no temporary substitute.

We always had dinner about one o'clock on Saturdays, soon after we came home from shul. After dinner my parents would take a nap and we children would be left to read in the dining room (which was also the living room). On a winter's day when we had a maid, we would sit round a roaring fire and read, helping ourselves at regular intervals from a large bag of boiled sweets which Mother provided every weekend; they came from Cooper's, the large Edinburgh grocers with branches all over the city, and were technically known as "Cooper's finest boilings," a description we considered expressive and appropriate. When there was no maid, we would huddle round a small electric radiator which would warm only those parts of the body immediately in front of it. I don't think I have ever been so cold as I have been sitting reading in our unheated house in Edinburgh on a winter Saturday afternoon. On one such afternoon I was reading an account of R. F. Scott's final and fatal expedition to the Antarctic, and the coldness of the scene described in the book mingled with the coldness of

[35]

the room to produce in me the impression that I was slowly freezing to death, and it was a long time before I felt really warm again. The South Pole, Cooper's finest boilings, and the coldness of our dining room are still connected in my imagination.

The electric radiator—which did, I suppose, make some difference, though memory links it only with extreme cold —could be switched on and off on the Sabbath, as the electric light also could, in accordance with a decision of my father's which differentiated his position sharply from that of my grandfather, patriarchal rabbi of an orthodox Jewish congregation in Leeds, who would have been shocked if he had known how cavalierly we treated electricity. Gas light or heat, which required the striking of a match, was another matter: that was clearly prohibited. But electricity was a phenomenon unrecognized by the Talmud, and my father felt free to make his own interpretation of the nature of the act of switching on the electric light or heat. He decided that it was not technically "kindling a fire," which a Biblical injunction prohibits in the home on the Sabbath.

The coldness of maidless winter Saturdays I took to be a part of the nature of things, and it never occurred to me to complain or rebel, or to feel in any degree sorry for myself. It seems to me now that I accepted a great deal of physical discomfort as a child with extraordinary equanimity: perhaps all children do and always have done. In the wintertime the bottoms of my short trousers would rub against the insides of my legs, above the knee, causing a painful irritation that lasted for months, and which sometimes became so acute that walking was most uncomfortable. But I never mentioned this to anybody, and I am sure that my mother never knew anything about it. It was part of winter,

[36]

like getting up at seven o'clock in an icy-cold bedroom and proceeding to have a cold bath (which I had been told was good for the physique). Every winter morning began with that tremendous summoning of the will to enable me to leave the beatific warmth of my bed for the cold linoleum floor of the chill bedroom; time never made it any easier; it was always an act of tremendous resolution, worked up with enormous effect. Yet it never occurred to me that the situation was anything to complain of, and the notion that bedrooms might be heated (except in cases of illness) would have struck me as bizarre in the extreme if I had ever heard of it, which I hadn't. Exercising the will became almost an obsession with me during parts of my childhood. Nobody compelled me to have cold baths on winter mornings—Lionel, though he started when I did, soon gave them up—but I felt that I had to challenge myself to keep on having them without any interruption (except on Sabbath mornings, when one never took a bath), and the more I was tempted to skip it for this one morning the more fiercely something inside me compelled me to go through with it.

In spite of these cold occasions, memories of light and warmth and festivity predominate in my recollections of childhood. Jewish family life makes much of the domestic festival, and the lighted candles, the large clean white tablecloth, the abundant food, made every Sabbath and festival eve a celebratory occasion. We would often have visitors, especially on Friday nights, and these visitors might be anybody. I remember Persian businessmen, American Rotarians, Zionist publicists from all parts of the world, a Swedish industrialist, a Palestinian student of veterinary surgery, Congressman Sol Bloom and his daughter on their way home from Switzerland, where the Congressman pressed (in vain) the claims of his reformed

[37]

calendar on the appropriate committee of the League of Nations, and lecturers and preachers galore. Every visitor to Edinburgh who had any Jewish connection at all seemed sooner or later to be having dinner with us, and the result was that Lionel and Sylvia and I were early accustomed to take completely for granted the presence at a meal of an odd or distinguished visitor. And in spite of my father's dignity of character and tendency to formality in speech, he was always tolerant of our interruptions, allowing us a remarkably free conversational play among the guests, so that from our tenderest years we would argue cheerfully with world-famous philosophers and dispute the confident generalizations of authoritative scholars. Talk was neither rationed nor disciplined in our family: it seems to me that we talked pretty nearly all the time. Lionel and Sylvia and I were always arguing; we would argue with our parents whenever we got the chance; and when there were visitors we took it for granted that we would argue with them. We were thus accustomed from our earliest years to accept lively conversation as a normal part of living—a civilized point of view that far too few people share.

As we grew older, we would argue about religion with our father, pressing him to defend the value of certain aspects of Jewish ritual or to explain the morality of certain actions of Biblical heroes. I remember once being struck by the fact that the phrase "the fear of Heaven and the fear of sin" occurs in a certain Hebrew prayer, denoting two desirable qualities in the good man, and though the English translation differentiated between the two "fears" by translating the first as "fear" and the second as "dread," the Hebrew word was the same, *yirath*, in each case. I asked my father once at dinner—I think I was twelve years old at the time—whether we were really supposed to

[38]

adopt the same attitude toward God as we were to adopt toward sin, and when he replied that the word had a different sense in each case I was far from satisfied and vehemently protested against the misleading of people by such loose diction. On another occasion I objected to the holding up of Abraham's willingness to sacrifice Isaac as something virtuous (this Biblical story still horrifies me); it was a revolting thing that Abraham had been asked to do, and the only proper conclusion for him to draw, if he thought that God was in earnest, was that this was not God speaking at all, but some evil spirit. And all three of us children were continually urging our father to preach against specific things we disliked in the behavior of the Jews of Edinburgh rather than produce grand and eloquent orations about Judaism in general. Not that we disapproved of the grand, eloquent orations; we were thrilled by them and proud of our father for being able to produce them; but we were—all three of us, I think—frequently bothered by the problem of the relation of ritual to practical ethics. We would press the claims of moral behavior over ritual scrupulousness, and would indignantly argue that it was much worse morally to engage in dubious business practices than to fail to go to synagogue regularly. (Fundamentally, I think my father agreed with us on this, and he was much concerned with the honor and civic virtue of the members of the Edinburgh Jewish community, but he considered it a major part of his duty to safeguard the integrity of the Jewish tradition, and ritual observance was of the first importance in keeping that tradition alive and in fostering a Jewish religious consciousness.)

We were not, at this stage, in rebellion, nor did we have the slightest sympathy with rebellion or even lax observance in others; we fully accepted orthodoxy and all its implications in daily practice, and we admired our father and were sure that he was always right. But we felt the need to ventilate with him all points that puzzled or annoyed us, and, oddly enough (though not really oddly, if one considers the atmosphere that prevailed in our family), he never took our arguments and objections as signs of backsliding or even of doubt about orthodoxy. Those who do not know what it is to have grown up in a family both highly orthodox and highly critical might find it hard to understand this combination of freedom of discussion with rigidity of behavior; to me it seems the most natural thing in the world, even now, when I am far from my childhood position on these matters. As often as not, my father would listen smilingly to our arguments or expressions of indignation, as though amused at the enthusiasm of youth, and would answer in perfect good humor. As the years went by, we gradually forced from him in argument a fairly complete system of Jewish apologetics, and I am sure that this helped him enormously in lecturing to students (which he often did) and meeting the arguments they presented in discussion after the lecture.

Sometimes he would get into violent arguments with brash young men who heckled him after one of his lectures at the Jewish Literary Society or the University Jewish Society. I remember a Russian student, called Krom, who took a militant atheist-communist line and had no inhibitions at all about expressing his contempt for religion and for the whole middle-class way of life. Though my father was admirable at expounding lucidly and persuasively his own particular brand of Jewish religious humanism ("I didn't know that Judaism was so utilitarian" was the dry comment of one of his hecklers after he had explained that only within a religious tradition and in relation to a divinely inspired code of morals could men lead truly full and satisfying lives) he was less good in the quick give-and-take of argument from the floor. He was not a quick thinker, and he did not always see the precise point that was being made. In our own domestic arguments with him we children had often to press him and say: "Yes, but that's not what I meant. What I meant was . . ." But if his thinking was fairly slow, it was deep enough, and once he had thought a point out he could express it with deceptive clarity. Only occasionally, when we pressed him too hard, he would answer shortly that we would understand that when we were older. And he believed that we would. He himself must have had, I feel sure, his own philosophical doubts and objections, and had eventually worked out for himself a philosophy of orthodox Judaism which combined a Kantian ethic with a profound respect for the rabbinical tradition and achievement. I am sure now that he thought that our youthful questions would all eventually be resolved in some such synthesis, and it never seems to have occurred to him that the synthesis between Judaism and modern Western thought which he had worked out for himself—with its social implications as to how Jews could live in such a country as Britain at once part of the general community and apart from it—might not serve for another generation, nor did he see what an extraordinary state of unstable equilibrium his own position represented.

My father seemed to take for granted that his own vast knowledge of Hebrew and rabbinics and Jewish religious philosophy would somehow filter down to us without too much active effort on his part. His own strenuous youth, in which he absorbed two different streams of education with a completeness that has always astonished me, was part of a world he had put behind him; he did not seem to ex-

[41]

pect us to emulate his own extraordinary feats of academic endurance. We belonged to the modern Western world which he had trained himself to cope with and to which he had so thoroughly adjusted his own religious position without giving up anything material in Jewish orthodoxy. Our Jewish knowledge and traditions we would get as a matter of course, because we were Daicheses and his sons; our secular education we must work for. He thus took great interest in our schooling once it had passed the elementary stage and would talk to us about our progress in Latin and Greek and mathematics, throwing Greek quotations from the *Odyssey* at us to see if we could translate them or asking what proposition in Euclid we were working at.

True, he gave us Hebrew lessons, and as far as I can remember I was able to read Hebrew before I could read English (I suspect it was my mother who taught me to read both languages): I cannot recollect a time when the reading of Hebrew did not come automatically to me. But his lessons were unsystematic and sporadic, and were sometimes interrupted by urgent telephone calls or unexpected visitors. Every Friday night we sang, in the traditional intonation, the following Saturday's portion of the law and the prophets, and so learned the synagogue cantillation by a gradual process of familiarization—we never deliberately sat down to memorize it. From an early age I was able to sing any passage at sight. And I picked up Biblical Hebrew by translating hundreds of passages in no sort of order and with no sort of system; I just found myself eventually able to read with understanding almost any part of the Hebrew Bible. To this day, if I am asked (as I occasionally am) how much Hebrew I know, I find it difficult to answer: it has often turned out that I know more than I think I know.

Every now and again my father would decide that we did not know enough systematic Hebrew grammar and would bring in from his study a dusty copy of Gesenius's Hebrew grammar and ask us to memorize the paradigms of verbs. But he would never stay long at this sort of thing. In the same sporadic way he would decide suddenly that it was time Lionel and I learned some Talmud, and he would appear with one of the huge volumes and take us at a galloping pace through *Baba Mezia,* "the Middle Gate," with its famous opening deciding the proper legal procedure and judgment if two men simultaneously come across and seize upon a lost garment ("really seize it," comments Rashi in his commentary on the commentary on the legal core of the passage). Or he would have a spell at medieval Hebrew poetry, or at Rashi's commentary on the Pentateuch (by some odd freak of memory I can still reel off the opening sentences of Rashi on Genesis); and once he thrust on me a Hebrew translation of Eugene Sue's *Mysteries of Paris.* He always professed himself surprised that we did not know more than we did, forgetting that since he was our teacher the responsibility was his. Once he suddenly said to me at dinner: "If you were hiking in Palestine and wanted to find a place to spend the night, how would you explain yourself in Hebrew to a passer-by?" And he laughed with a mixture of good nature and reproof when I said *"hayesh po makom lagur"* (is there here a place to sojourn?) instead of *"hayesh po makom lalun"* (is there here a place to lodge for the night?).

At one point my mother, distressed at the lack of system in my father's teaching of us, which she attributed to his being too busy to attend to the matter properly, insisted that Lionel and I should receive regular lessons from a professional Hebrew teacher. My father, who had refused

[43]

to send us to the cheder, the regular Hebrew school attached to the synagogue, of which he was headmaster, on the grounds that we knew it all anyway and further that the rabbi's sons should not have to go to cheder, resisted this proposal for a long time, but at length found a young Hebrew teacher who, in return for weekly lessons in rabbinics from my father, agreed to give my brother and me regular and systematic Hebrew lessons. As far as I remember, these lessons went on for about a year, and were the most systematic we ever had. We wrote regular prose compositions in modern Hebrew, and learned our grammar thoroughly. The teacher, whose name was Abraham Chayim Gordon but whom my brother and I called Aby Chayim and mocked mercilessly, was a small man with a dark mustache and an excitable manner, much given to extraordinary digressions on questions of law and logic. He once tried to convince us that, just as two negatives make a positive, so two positives make a negative, and that is why (he alleged), when an overeager witness replies "yes, yes" in answer to a question put to him instead of simply "yes," Jewish law discounts his affirmative reply. Lionel and I tried hard to explain to him that logically a second affirmative could only reaffirm the first, and couldn't possibly negate it, but he remained adamant in his conviction that "yes, yes" was equivalent logically to "no." It seemed to me then, as it does now, that overeagerness in a witness should rightly be regarded with suspicion, without the implication that a double positive makes a negative. Aby Chayim also enunciated the theory (but only as a possibility) that the name "Shylock" in *The Merchant of Venice* derived from the Hebrew verb *"shaál,"* to ask, presumably because people were always asking Shylock for money. When I suggested this to my father, he replied brusquely, "Non-

[44]

sense!" Aby Chayim was very patient with us, and took our mockery in good part, and when after a while he left for America we were sorry to see him go. But I think my father was glad when he went, not because he did not respect his ability as a Hebrew teacher, but because he resented the fact that his sons should have to have Hebrew lessons from somebody else.

When I was about twelve, my father began a series of Sunday morning lectures on the Hebrew prophets to the older boys and girls of his congregation, and as this was a more advanced course than anything taught in the cheder he decided that my brother and I ought to go. These lectures, which were based on the Hebrew text, consisted of an *explication de texte* interspersed with some general comments. Rather to my surprise, my father also insisted on the class memorizing whole chapters of Isaiah, and offered a prize to the pupil who could memorize most. For some reason, in spite of my generally bad memory, I found it easy to memorize the rich, sounding Hebrew of the "deutero-Isaiah" (though to my father there was only one Isaiah) and, starting with the magnificent chapter 40, learned by heart most of the remainder of the book. I forced myself to keep memorizing more and more, and derived a strange excitement from doing so. Every night as I lay in bed before falling asleep I would repeat to myself as much as I had yet learned. It was not for the sake of the prize that I did this, although I naturally expected that the prize would go to me, since I knew that nobody else in the class had memorized so much. It never occurred to me that my father would be embarrassed at having to give the prize to his own son, and I was indignant and hurt when, at the end of the term, he announced that the winner was a certain boy who had memorized about half of what I had and, further, always recited it in what sounded to me like a horrid, expressionless monotone. I was announced as having come second, equal with a girl who had memorized the first part of chapter 40 and recited it in an adenoidal singsong which completely ruined the sonority of the Hebrew. The grand opening of the chapter (*Nachamu, nachamu ami,"* "Comfort ye, comfort ye my people") she would pronounce "Dechebu, dechebu abi," as though she had a heavy cold and at the same time was trying to be very genteel. The girl was known as "Dechebu Dechebu" in our family ever after that.

That was in 1925, the year of the opening of the Hebrew University in Jerusalem. My father was invited to take part in the ceremony, and was most anxious to go, but he could not possibly afford it. At the last moment one of the wealthier members of his congregation generously offered to stand my father the trip, an offer which was gratefully accepted. This was the happy springtime of the Zionist movement, and my father, a pioneer Zionist with a high idealistic belief in the glories of a restored Zion, was excited and inspired to an extraordinary degree by his visit. He gave many lectures on conditions in Palestine on his return, and it was clear that, whatever less sympathetic eyes had observed, he had seen nothing but healthy, enthusiastic, and pious young men and women building up their ancestral home. He was never the kind of Zionist who believed that all Jews ought to settle in Palestine or that Jewish life outside Palestine was doomed to decline as Zionist ideals were realized: he believed that a rebuilt Jewish national home would be a source of strength and religious inspiration to the Jews of the rest of the world. His real ambition was to see Palestine become not only a Jewish state but also a British dominion, an integral part of the British Empire—a posi-

tion which was held by some influential English political
figures, led by Colonel Josiah Wedgwood (later Lord
Wedgwood), who wrote a book, entitled *The Seventh
Dominion*, strongly advocating such a development. Any
friction between Zionists and the British Government was
a source of bitter disappointment to my father, who had
known and admired Lord Balfour, and the events of the
1940's shook him severely. He was shocked by the extreme
position taken by some vocal American Zionists in those
later years and by their tendency to condone terrorism, and
at the same time he was hurt and disappointed at the behavior of the British Government. At the time of his death,
in 1945, he had moved a considerable distance away from
the Zionist orthodoxy of the day and was more concerned
with the position of Jews outside Palestine.

But in 1925 nothing of this was visible on the horizon,
and my father's visit to Palestine was in many respects the
high point of his career. He was invited to be present (if my
recollection of his account of his trip has not become confused) at the laying of the foundation stone of the new Tel
Aviv synagogue, and boasted that when he was unexpectedly asked to make a speech (in modern Hebrew) he
was able to give an eloquent, spontaneous oration which
drew great applause. The ceremony was held on the eighth
day of Passover, which was observed as a festival day (when
no work could be done) by those Jews who came from outside Palestine, because doubt about the calendar had, at an
early stage of the Jewish dispersion, led Jews of the
galuth (exile) to observe an extra day in order to be on
the safe side; but it was not observed by those Jews who
lived in Palestine, for whom Passover had concluded the
day before. The result was that the Jews from abroad,
like my father, were unable to ride or write or work on

that day, while the Jews of Tel Aviv went about their daily affairs in the normal way. Some of those attending the ceremony at the synagogue were thus still in festival mood, and others were not. My father used to talk about this with an amused air, as reflecting an interesting facet of modern Jewish life; he noted also that it meant that he, unlike the other speakers on this occasion, who lived in Palestine, was unable to write down notes for his speech and would have had to deliver it without notes even if he had not preferred to do so anyway.

Everything on this Palestine expedition seemed to go well. The only fly in the ointment was that he was accompanied throughout his visit by a somewhat eccentric gentleman, an Edinburgh Christadelphian, who professed himself a great friend of the Jews and an ardent Zionist. This gentleman (who tacked himself on to my father in order to make sure that he would have the entree to all the proper places) was a great bore who enjoyed the sound of his own voice and edited (or perhaps only distributed in Scotland) a strange magazine called *Glad Tidings of the Coming Age,* which he sent regularly to my father. He used to make speeches to Jewish audiences in Edinburgh in which he announced that he was converted to Zionism in Norfolk, Virgina, where someone had once said to him: "If there is anything of the milk of human kindness in you, you will become a Zionist." Apparently he found this argument so convincing that he became a Zionist forthwith. He frequented Jewish homes in Edinburgh and occasionally came to the synagogue; his Jewish contacts resulted in his picking up a few Hebrew words, which he tended to pronounce with the letters transposed, spooneristically, as it were. He would call *shekolim* (shekels; specifically, in Zionist usage, the silver coin—in Britain, half a crown—

which each Zionist paid to the movement in token of his membership) *shelokim,* and would make speeches about *shelokim* on Zionist platforms. He was an object of ribald mirth among the Jewish youth of Edinburgh, and was something of a thorn in my father's flesh as he tagged around after him in Palestine. Jews are vulnerable to that kind of lunatic pro-Semitism; they cannot afford to reject it, but its acceptance is often embarrassing.

A more congenial pro-Semitic gentile in Edinburgh was the white-bearded Mr. Hogg, a kindly old man who would attend the synagogue fairly frequently and was on friendly terms with many Jewish families. Once at a children's Chanukah party he asked one of the young guests what Chanukah was all about, expecting to hear the familiar story of Judas Maccabeus and the rededication of the Temple, and was horrified when the child replied: "Chanukah is the Jews' Christmas." The story was told as a joke among the Jews of Edinburgh, but I remember my father looked thoughtful when he heard it: did it suggest, perhaps, the instability of his synthesis?

We used to have quite a number of non-Jewish visitors to the synagogue, mostly Presbyterian ministers and divinity students. Many of them would take off their hats as they entered, to the scandal of the congregation, who would motion the offending gentile to replace his hat, sometimes gesturing so violently that the poor man would be quite confused and not know what he was supposed to do. (Orthodox Jews, of course, always cover their heads when they pray or engage in biblical or Talmudic study). I was quick to notice these visitors, and to resent for their sake the lack of decorum and haphazard out-of-time singing so characteristic of an orthodox Jewish congregation. I would wish that everyone would behave with a ritual solemnity so

[49]

as to impress the newcomer. It was years later that I learned to understand and appreciate the ease and individualism with which the Orthodox Jew conducts himself in the presence of his Maker, and to resent not the lack of decorum in orthodox congregations but the artificial stiffness and coldness of certain less orthodox services. As a child I was always annoyed by the lack of manners displayed by the older members of my father's congregation, and my father, too, worked hard to improve the discipline of the service. He at least put a stop to the continuous walking in and out and the perpetual chattering, but even he could not get the older men to suspend their individualistic habits, such as singing one bar ahead of the chazan to show that they knew the words and music better than he did, or engaging in loud private prayer during what was supposed to be a hushed pause in the service.

One thing, however, I was never ashamed of when there was a visitor present, and that was my father's sermon. When my father moved into the pulpit to preach, I would say to myself: *"Now* he'll see what a Jewish rabbi can do," and I would watch the visitor's face for signs that he was moved and impressed as my father spoke. And my father never let me down: he was a great preacher, and, without the aid of any kind of note, could build up from exposition of the day's text through illustrative anecdote to a climax of eloquence I have rarely heard equalled. He gave out the text in Hebrew, and then translated it into English, continuing his sermon in the latter language. Sometimes, on a chill winter afternoon when there were not more than a dozen people present, most of them old men whose command of the English language was rudimentary, I would feel that nobody except myself understood or appreciated his preaching, and a sense of the waste of it all would press sadly upon me. My father preached every Sabbath, however small the congregation might be; and his sermon was always perfectly constructed, always cogently and eloquently expressed, always sounding with true moral passion. Only once do I remember his not preaching (apart from the very few occasions when he was absent through illness); and that was on a cold February morning when the primitive central heating apparatus had broken down and there was barely a minyan (ten men) present. On that occasion he reluctantly decided to let his shivering congregation go home twenty minutes earlier than usual, and did not preach. I said to him on the way home that I missed his sermon, and I remember his sudden pleased smile as he turned to me and said: "Did you?"

CHAPTER 3

In March, 1919, at the age of six and a half, I went with my father to interview Mr. John Alison, headmaster of George Watson's Boys' College, Edinburgh. The interview was satisfactory, and the same day (unless my memory telescopes the events) I took my seat in Class "B" of the elementary department. The classroom was tucked away in the extreme corner of the right wing of the school building; you had to turn into a small L-shaped recess in order to get there. The characteristic school smell—it seemed to be a mixture of wood, chalk, leather (from schoolbags), ink (the school ink was almost black and had a pungent odor), and the monastic coolness which emanated from the stone-floored corridors—assailed my nostrils as I came in at the main entrance with my father, up the wide steps by the portico and the fluted columns, past the janitor's room where we were directed to the headmaster by a uniformed official with twinkling blue eyes and a small white beard. (I was to know him well later; he was Willie, the senior janitor, good friend to all the small boys of Watson's. Fairlie, the junior janitor, was of more unpredictable temper. The fact that Fairlie was universally known by his surname while Willie was just Willie to everybody indicated a

significant difference in their characters. Willie retired halfway through my school career at Watson's, and for years
afterward I used to see the brisk old man with a single golf
club in his hand—a cleek—on his way to Bruntsfield Links
to knock a ball round the simple nine-hole free golf course
there.)

I found the work in Class "B" easy enough, for I could
already read and write and do simple sums with slapdash
speed, but it took me some time to get used to the formality
and regularity of the classroom. For some reason, the idea of
starting work promptly at nine o'clock each morning distressed me, and I explained to Miss Don, the teacher, that
I did not think I should be able to manage it. She smiled,
and said that I must do my best, and I earnestly replied that
I would. Shortly afterward, Miss Don left to get married
and her place was taken by Miss Barron or Miss Barrons, a
name which the boys in the class for some reason found
themselves unable to enunciate clearly. Miss Barn, Miss
Barmy, and Miss Barley were favorite variants, and I remember myself that when I first heard her called Miss
Barley I decided at once that that was the simplest and most
convenient form of the name and that I would therefore
stick to it. I do not think that there was any deliberate
mockery involved in this playing about with Miss Barron's
name: "Barron" just seemed to be difficult or at least
implausible.

In the autumn of 1919 I moved up to Class "D," taught
by one of the numerous Miss Smiths at Watson's. She was
popularly known among the boys as "Smiggles o' D," which
distinguished her from "Smiggles of H," the Miss Smith
who was to teach me the following year when I moved up
into Class "H." Smiggles o' D was an old war horse of a
teacher, who had got the teaching of seven- and eight-year-

olds systematized into a well-tried routine. She was efficient in a tired sort of way, and had a cut-and-dried list of basic offenses for which punishment by the "tawse" (a leather strap, used on the palm of the hand) was obligatory. If, for example, you handed in your writing exercise (which was done at home) smudged and filthy with dirty finger marks you got the tawse. And of course you got the tawse for cheating. One morning, after she had marked the sums that we had been doing in class, she discovered that both I and the boy sitting next to me had got one sum wrong, and that we both had the same wrong answer. She decided that I had copied my answer from the boy beside me. This decision outraged me, for in fact I had not copied the answer, and I was better at arithmetic than the boy whom she assumed I had copied from. She insisted that the evidence proved that I had cheated, yet, since she refrained from giving me the tawse and contented herself with a tongue lashing, she must have realized that there was just as much chance of the other boy's having cheated. (As a matter of fact, I was convinced then and I still am that neither of us cheated: our getting the same wrong answer was simply a coincidence.) Throughout the rest of the day she would interrupt what she was saying to refer to me as the boy who had cheated. After a while I ceased to deny it, and, with the extraordinary resilience of childhood, shrugged the whole thing off. But I knew from that moment that Miss Smith was a wickedly irresponsible woman, and I never forgave her. I cannot bring myself to forgive her yet, though she has been dead now for some years. She destroyed forever my trust in teachers.

The following year, when I was in Class "H," I really did cheat, in a curiously lighthearted way without any sense of sin. Why I did it still puzzles me. One day I could not be bothered memorizing my geography homework, so I carefully wrote out the names of the rivers and the populations of the cities and the other facts and figures I was expected to learn by heart, and when next morning we were asked to write down the answers to questions on these matters I quietly took out the piece of paper on which I had written down the answers and copied them into my exercise book. As far as I can remember, I made no great effort to conceal what I was doing, and congratulated myself on having discovered a simple and efficient way of getting good marks. Of course I was soon spotted, and Smiggles of H was horrified at my criminal behavior—all the more criminal because I was regarded as a bright boy who had no need of such wicked tricks. I got two strokes of the tawse—my first experience of that instrument of torture—and was sent to the bottom of the class. I felt neither worried nor aggrieved, moving through the whole experience in a sort of trance, but I was astonished at the amount of real pain inflicted by the tawse and by the length of time it lasted. For over half an hour my hand felt as thought it were about a foot thick and the tips of my fingers, which felt as large as balloons, pulsed with agony. Then suddenly the pain changed into a warm glow, and everything was very pleasant. I never bore any grudge against Smiggles of H; she was, of course, only doing her duty.

My father, satisfied that he had started my brother Lionel and me at a good school, took little interest in the details of our secular education in these early years. This was partly because he was too busy: these were the years when he was licking his congregation into shape and establishing himself in Edinburgh and throughout Scotland as an important public figure and recognized spokesman for the Jewish point of view; and it was at this time, too, that my mother had her serious illness. Another reason for his relative indifference to what we were doing in the elementary school at Watson's was that he had nothing to say about this stage of our education. He was waiting until he could cap quotations from Homer with us or ask what book of Virgil we were reading, or for that still later stage when he could inquire whether we had read Buckle on the history of civilization or David Hume on human nature. He did, however, appear at the annual school prize-giving, in dignified black coat and silk hat, to have a few grave words with Dr. Alison (he became "Dr. Alison" in, I think, 1922, when Edinburgh University granted him an honorary LL.D.) and thank him for what the school was doing for "my boys."

Watson's was divided into three sections, the elementary school, the junior school, and the senior school. I entered the junior school at the age of nine, after leaving Class "H." Here we still had one teacher for all subjects, and for the first two years they were still women teachers. But in the autumn of 1923, when I entered the third year of the junior school, I came under the redoubtable "Dub-Dub," Mr. W. W. Anderson, a man with a reputation throughout the school as a stern disciplinarian and a teacher of old-fashioned strictness and thoroughness. He was within a few years of retirement when I came to know him as a teacher, a dour old Scot with a gray and ginger mustache and very little hair. His methods were old-fashioned, but remarkably effective. He battered the boys with a brand of irony all his own, and after bellowing at one of them for some error or piece of forgetfulness he would lean back against the mantel and say sardonically: "You think I'm hard on you, don't you? You think I'm a Turk? You think I'm a Tartar? You're going to complain to your parents about me?" He would then pause and remove his gold-rimmed pince-nez glasses. "Go home and tell your mother I'm a Tartar. Tell her I'm a Turk." And he would give a curious little sibilant titter which sounded like "sih, sih, sih."

Dub-Dub never used the "tawse," but he had his own way of keeping discipline. He was more feared, I think, than any other master in the school, and it was rumored among the boys that he was not allowed to use the strap because once, away back in the 1880's or '90's, he had broken a boy's wrist with it. But I doubt if this was true. His moods of sternness made one tremble, and his levity had something of the quality of a jocund rattlesnake. He could get the most extraordinary effects out of the simplest sentences. If he threatened (as he occasionally did) to throw a boy out of the classroom, he would say, in a peculiarly intense intonation, "I'll change your name to Walker." That threat, with its monstrous pun (it meant "I'll make you walk out of the room") always hushed a class to immediate stillness. "Change it to Walker," he'd repeat, meditatively. Then, suddenly: "Give your dear mother my compliments and tell her I'm a Turk."

He taught by slogans, rhyming tags, and rules chanted to the accompaniment of a waved pointer. (Do all school-teachers employ the pointer to the extent that the Watson's teachers did in those days? It was their favorite weapon, and I have a mental image of every one of them, each holding the pointer in his favorite attitude, one pointing to a wall map, another waving it in the air, a third banging it on the floor, a fourth following the lines of some geometrical figure on the blackboard with it, a fifth poking it in an inattentive boy's stomach. And one senior teacher used to lay it across his back and wrap his arms round it, wrestling with it and himself as he talked.) One of Dub-Dub's favorite

[57]

grammatical rules was that which postulates the nominative case after the verb "to be," and if anybody said, for example, *"Marcus est puerum"* instead of *"Marcus est puer"* he would at once break into a wild chant, waving his pointer at the offender, and digging it into his stomach at the end:

> Before and after the verb "to be"
> The very same cases I shall see—
> IF I keep my eyes open.

He was intensely proud of being Scottish, but his Scotland was not that of the sentimental Jacobites or of the modern Scots Nationalists. The view of Scottish history that he taught us was the Calvinist-Nationalist one. No nonsense about Mary Queen of Scots or Bonnie Prince Charlie for him; it was the Covenanters and the Battle of Bothwell Brig and the horrid persecutions of Bloody Claverhouse that we learned about. We had to memorize the oath that the Covenanters took, and were liable to be called upon to recite it at any time. Though his geographical interests were wide, and we were expected to know a great deal about French rivers ("the Rhône joins the *Sone* [Saone] at *Lyone* [Lyon]" was one of his rhyming tags) and German towns, history for him was always and only Scottish history, and almost exclusively the history of the Covenanters at that. The only boy's book that won his approval was R. M. Ballantyne's *Hunted and Harried* (less well known in its day than the same author's *Coral Island*), which dealt in a tone of idealizing sympathy with the sufferings of the upholders of the true Kirk. I persuaded my father that it was one of our required schoolbooks, so that he bought it for me; I carried it around with me at school conspicuously, and Dub-Dub nodded approval.

[58]

Dub-Dub had an elaborate system of marking his pupils. The order in which you sat in class was determined by how well you did, and at the end of the day he gave five marks to the boy sitting at the top, four marks to the second boy, three to the third, two to the fourth, and one to the fifth. The next day the previous day's five top boys moved right down to the bottom (whence, of course, they tried to work their way up to the top again) and everybody else moved up automatically five places. The competition was tremendous, and the movements up and down continuous. Dub-Dub would shoot a question at the class, starting with the top boy and going down until he could find a boy who answered it correctly (and immediately); that boy would then go up top, and everybody else between the winning boy's original seat and the top would move down one. "Take him down!" he would roar, as two or three boys missed a question and he came to one who got it right. He would give you only a split second to answer. Pouncing anywhere in the class his pointer would travel down, "Next, next, next —right! Take him down!" A "taking down" session was liable to start at any moment throughout the school day, and sometimes the excitement was furious. Dub-Dub particularly enjoyed humiliating a bright boy. He would wait until one of these was momentarily dozing or looking out of the window and lunge at him with his pointer. "Accusative plural of *acies*. Next, next, next—TAKE HIM DOWN!"

This was more than sport, for one's weekly marks depended in considerable measure on one's daily place in class, and out of one's weekly marks (together with periodical tests and examinations) was figured one's final position in class at the end of the year. The boys in the top half-dozen positions got book prizes, and the boy at the very top got a scholarship, which meant that his parents had no fees to pay during the following year. It was in Dub-Dub's class that I first became fully sensible of the tremendously competitive atmosphere of a Scottish school. The curriculum and the teaching were really organized for the boys at the top of the class, and at every test and examination relative positions were worked out and hopes rose and fell. More than half of the class were out of the battle; they lived a more relaxed and I suppose a happier life, content if they could keep abreast of the work sufficiently to be promoted into a higher class at the end of the year. But for those in the running for awards, the competition was keen and unremitting.

Of course there were other ways of winning fame at school, notably on the rugby field. But that way was completely closed to me, not because I was naturally incompetent at sports (though I never liked organized games of any kind) but because games were played on Saturday, the Jewish Sabbath, and my playing then was quite out of the question. I suppose I could have found a way of taking part in practices while not playing in matches, but my father's complete lack of awareness of this side of school life, and his tacit assumption that school was where one learned the orthodox academic subjects and nothing else, prevented this. Not for him any notion that games built up character: his children's characters would be formed by the atmosphere of a Jewish home, and the school had no responsibility for that. He was simply puzzled or bored if anyone showed interest in competitive sport. Exercise was another matter. He believed in taking long walks over the hills; he understood and approved when, during my university days, I went with my fellow students for rambles over the Pentland Hills or spent part of the holidays hiking in the

Highlands; swimming, too, he considered healthful, and golf was an exercise that both promoted health and gave one the opportunity of moving among fine scenery. But rugby or cricket did not exist for him, and so he assumed that they did not exist for his children.

It would not be strictly true to say that I resented this; it was a situation that I took absolutely for granted, as part of the natural order of things. I had no great desire to play rugger or cricket, but I did at times feel embarrassed at being the only boy in my class who was totally ignorant even of the terminology connected with these games. And I knew nothing about the school matches: they were nearly all played on Saturdays, and Lionel and I rarely saw one. But my mother, so much more sensitive to this aspect of school life than my father, realized that we were missing something and always found out from the local paper whenever a match was scheduled to be played on a weekday. She would give us the information and pack us off to Myreside, the school playing field. In this way we sometimes saw the opening of the Watsonians (Watson's former pupils) against Hillhead F.P.'s, generally played, if I remember rightly, on the first Thursday before the opening of the autumn term. And sometimes a match was postponed because of the weather or some other reason, and we would get a half-holiday on a Wednesday to go to see the replay: the whole school would troop out to Myreside, and Lionel and I would follow, not quite knowing what it was all about—indeed not at first knowing where Myreside was, something we dared not admit as we blindly followed the crowd—but trying to look nonchalant and well informed. We could not enter for the annual School Sports either, because this great event was also held on a Saturday. It was only late in my school career that I discovered that I was a good sprinter, and could outrun many of my school-fellows who had some reputation as athletes. But there was nothing I could do about it.

There was one compensating factor, however. It was during my year in Dub-Dub's class that I had begun to amuse myself by writing crude and highly derivative verses. I found that I had a certain facility in handling rhyme and meter, and in the imitative way of childhood I turned out a number of descriptions of imaginary moonlit scenes and similar things. It never occurred to me at this time that this was in the least interesting or unusual, that it was any different from scribbling in a drawing book or playing a parlor game: I remember my astonishment at discovering some years later, when our English teacher set us a verse-writing competition, that most of the boys in my class found difficulty in putting a thought into rhymed, metrical verse. If occasionally I read out one of my poems to the family, I did so in the same casual way that one might show a trick with a matchbox or demonstrate that one could now turn a proper somersault. It was generally humorous poems that I read to the family, like "The Rime of the Ancient Scavenger" and a set of Lewis Carroll-like nonsense verses entitled "The Polywagoo." In my next to last year at school I translated the first book of the *Odyssey* into limerick verse. All I remember now is the opening:

> O Muse, tell to me of the chap
> Who wandered all over the map.
>   This remarkable boy
>   After bashing down Troy
> Started off on a tour of mishap.

It was done in the same spirit as other boys made catapults or collected cigarette cards.

It was my father who first began to take my verses seriously. When I was eleven years old he bought me a notebook in which to write out fair copies, and after I had gone to bed he would solemnly read what I had written there and make minor corrections to improve the regularity of the meter (and once, I remember, to correct the grammar). One evening he sat down with me and gave me a lesson in metrics, explaining to me about the various feet, and writing out metrical schemes with ‿'s and dashes (‿ — ‿ —). He had the strictest notions of poetic rhythm, and knew nothing of the doctrine of equivalence or the sprung rhythm theories of Hopkins. Nevertheless, his discipline was helpful to me at the time: it gave me a sense of technical craftsmanship and chastened my uncontrolled exuberance. It also gave me a bias in favor of metrical regularity which persists to this day.

One day, without my knowledge, my father brought my notebook of poems to school and showed it to Dr. Alison, who referred him to Mr. Findlay ("Henry John"), the head of the English department in the senior school. Mr. Findlay liked some of the poems, and chose one ("To a fountain in moonlight," describing in a fairly complicated verse form a scene I had never witnessed) to print in *The Watsonian,* the school magazine. *The Watsonian* was a dull, businesslike magazine, with contributions by masters and by senior boys; unlike some school magazines, it had no children's section in which to print crude and amusing effusions by youngsters. My poem, therefore, was not printed as an amusing or psychologically interesting example of a child's versifying: it was printed as a poem in its own right. I was both pleased and embarrassed. It was embarrassing to have my father talking about my poems and showing them to teachers, and it was even embarrassing, in

[63]

a way, to see something from my private notebook in print, to be read by my schoolfellows. But of course I was also immensely proud—proud of my printed poem, and proud of my father's interest in my verses.

Dub-Dub was not impressed. One day, after the appearance of the issue of *The Watsonian* which contained my poem, he found me looking dreamily out of the window and at once proceeded to catch me out in a "taking down" session. After my humiliation he growled at me: "I hope you're not letting all this poetry stuff addle your brains and keep you from your proper work." The class tittered, and I was profoundly hurt.

I was eleven years old then, and the next year I moved up to the senior school, where the organization was quite different and we had a different master for each subject. We started science this year (with physics) and French and algebra and geometry, and in history for the first time we moved away from Scotland to get a wider perspective. It was now that I began to prefer some subjects to others: English, history, and languages were my favorites, while mathematics (except algebra, which for some reason I liked and was reasonably good at) and physics (which was badly taught by the master we had then, though there were some excellent physics teachers in the school) I found on the whole rather dull. The first year of the senior school had I suppose about a hundred and forty boys, and they were divided into four groups: IA, a group of about thirty-five, contained the brightest boys, IB the next brightest, and IC the poorer pupils, while in I Mod (later called ID) were the boys who elected to take the "modern" side as a preparation for a nonprofessional future—in my time they were regarded as a pretty inferior lot. I was in IA, and the next year moved into IIA, and so on. Here the competition was extremely fierce, and for my first two years in the senior school I stayed about tenth—which meant missing a prize or a scholarship. Each time, I started the year determined that I would work really hard and come top of the class, but somehow that pristine keenness evaporated as the academic year progressed: I worked well at the subjects I liked, and tended to ignore the others.

In my third senior year we began Greek, which meant that I was now taking three languages, Latin, French, and Greek. (Normally, one had to choose at this stage between Greek and French, dropping the latter if one was taking up the former, but Mr. Robertson, the new headmaster who had succeeded Dr. Alison, tried an experiment this year: he had the brightest boys of the year—those in the A class—take both Greek and French, without giving them any choice.) This gave me an extra subject which I liked and was good at, and meant that out of the eight subjects I took I was top or near the top in five (English, history, Latin, Greek, and French), though I remained about the middle in the other three (science, mathematics, and geography). The result was that one exciting day early in July, 1927, I dashed home across the Meadows during the lunch interval to announce to my parents that I had won a "bursary"—that is, remission of fees for the ensuing year, together with a cash grant. I had not, in fact, come top of my class, for there were several bursaries available for the third year, and of course IIIA captured them all, but I had finally got into the scholarship category and I was immensely pleased and excited.

I was pleased on my own account, of course, but even more because I knew my parents would be gratified. At this time I had formed an image of my father as a lonely idealist who would be sustained by the knowledge that one at least of his children was of a similar habit of mind. (My brother Lionel took his schooling with a lazy matter-of-factness and was content to swim gently along in the middle of a B stream. It was much later that his specific talents —legal and rhetorical—began to display themselves.) I believed that if I could show my father signs that I was on the way to becoming a serious thinker and writer and linguist, or at any rate someone of moral and intellectual distinction, it would sweeten his whole life. As a matter of fact, I found myself developing an almost paternal attitude toward both my parents. Looking at them sitting by the fire on a Friday night, tired after a hard week's work, love and pity would well up within me and I wanted to say something that would give them tremendous pleasure.

It is easy to see why I felt protective toward my mother: she had had periods of serious illness and I felt that her arduous daily routine of housework might at any moment break her. On the rare occasions when she went out in the evening to some social function, I would lie awake in bed until she got safely home, thinking of her as someone too fragile to be out in the dark night, especially if there was a high wind or the weather was really cold. It is more surprising that I should have felt in a somewhat similar way toward my father, for he was a man of fine physique and great strength of character whom one would not for a moment have associated with any kind of weakness. Underneath this strength, however, I seemed to detect even at this early age a certain childlike quality of character, a naïve faith in the world, a simple conviction of the absolute rightness of his own position, that made me want to protect him from certain kinds of knowledge and to keep on reassuring him that the world was indeed as he saw it and we were all on his side. He knew nothing, I would some-

[66]

times feel, of the realities of the modern world, of its daily, trivial preoccupations. Could such a man know that schoolboys talked smut, that to many parents as well as to many boys sport meant more than study, that stealing notebooks from the janitors' cupboard at school was regarded by almost everybody as legitimate, that most people were silly, cruel, materialist, selfish? His eloquent and stirring sermons, which I so admired, did not really belong to the world in which I moved at school and in the Edinburgh streets. Could he know that the ritual of orthodox Judaism, so important and impressive to him (and to me), was comic or fatuous to many people? The thinker, the scholar, the idealist, were isolated characters, who had no part in the life of the rough mob. It was at this time that I refused to go to parties and preferred to sit at home and read poetry or go for lonely walks in which I worked myself up into a state of romantic exaltation. Lonely myself, feeling different from and (it must be admitted) superior to other people, I saw my father as another lonely hero, but one who was not really aware of his essential loneliness, one who did not know how different the world really was from his noble vision of it.

Looking back, it seems to me now that in some ways I exaggerated my father's innocence. He was in many respects remarkably tough-minded. He had an uncanny gift for recognizing impostors; and his duties as rabbi naturally brought him into contact with sordid aspects of, for example, marriage that as a child I knew nothing whatever about. Yet I still think that my general impression of him as an innocent and lonely idealist was essentially right. In spite of his knowledge of the seamy side of life, in spite of his shrewdness in detecting imposture and his toughness in handling dishonest appeals for charity, a certain childish optimism was central to his character. Another childish trait of his was a naïve susceptibility to flattery. Anybody could disarm him with a compliment. Though he found it hard to suffer fools gladly, a man who in all other ways appeared a fool could earn a reputation for wisdom with my father by telling him how much he admired his letters to the *Scotsman* or what a wonderful speaker he thought he was. I remember once, after I was grown up, arguing with him about the intelligence of a young man who had had occasion to visit the house and had talked a great deal of arrant nonsense. "Oh, he's not such a fool," my father said, and added, with a smile of reminiscent pleasure, "he said that my letters to the editor were the best things that ever appeared in the *Scotsman* and I ought to collect them in a book." There was something rather engaging about this simple kind of vanity.

There can be no doubt of my father's loneliness, though he would have been surprised to hear of it. His own work as rabbi and synthesizer of orthodox Jewish and British culture so engrossed him, both physically and mentally, that he had no time for the luxuries of friendship or society. His social life was crowded indeed, but it was part of his professional life, and the weddings, receptions, public meetings, official dinners, and similar functions which he attended in enormous numbers could hardly be put in the category of relaxation with friends. My impression was that the nearest he ever came to relaxing outside his own home was at Masonic dinners: he was a keen Mason, and enjoyed the meetings of Lodge Solomon (of which he was a Past Master), which included both Jewish and Christian members. But he had no real cronies. Throughout his whole adult life there was no one outside his immediate family with whom he was on first-name terms. There were several members of his congregation with whom he would enjoy a chat on community or general affairs. But there was no one with whom he was really intimate, no one who understood fully what he was trying to do, what his concept of Scottish-Jewish life was, what constituted the real center of his moral and emotional life. Even my mother hardly ever called him "Salis." She once told me that she was relieved when her first child was born because it solved the problem of what to call her husband, whom she felt shy of calling by his (admittedly somewhat unusual) first name: she called him "Daddy" more often than not from that time on. He always called her "Flora," with the "o" vowel rather clipped and short.

It was this sort of thing that I was becoming more and more aware of in my fifteenth year, which I look back on as a critical year in my development. I remember 1927—particularly the summer—with especial clarity. It was the year of my first bursary, the year of my growing sense of romantic isolation from my fellows, a year when I wrote a vast amount of derivative verse and cultivated moods of introspective melancholy. How can I explain the enormous sense of emotional excitement which used to overcome me as I sat on summer evenings by the window of the attic room Lionel and I used as a "study" and responded to the sights and sounds of Edinburgh life outside. I was the artist, pondering over the sad beauty of human destiny. When I read Wordsworth's phrase, "the still sad music of humanity," I thought I recognized at once what he meant. To this day I associate that phrase with my brooding over those summer evenings from my attic window in Millerfield Place. These experiences are not merely fragments that linger in my memory: they are as vivid today as they ever were, an important part of my self. But

[69]

though the memories are still vivid and important to me, the experience itself, which recurred frequently throughout my teens and my twenties, came less and less in my thirties and now, in my forties, I find that it has gone apparently for good.

It was in my fifteenth year, too, that I became aware of a difference in character and temperament between my mother and my father which led me to feel that I understood them both better than either understood the other, and I wished to interpret them to each other. I would imagine my father's youth and his student days in Germany (somehow always connected with a picture in a German reading book of a late nineteenth-century German railway station, with men in top hats and beards walking about or sitting waiting for a train: this picture seemed to me infinitely sad, suggesting a lost world and symbolizing in some oblique way the lonely self-dedication with which my father lived and worked in the years before I was born). I would think of my mother, the beautiful eldest daughter of a Liverpool Jewish family, musical, literary, accomplished, marrying my father at the age of nineteen in a splendor of idealistic hope that she would absorb his knowledge and power and the two would serve the great cause together. My mother's idealism was nineteenth-century romantic, while my father's was eighteenth-century sentimental, and in spite of their deep mutual affection there were important points on which they never really understood each other. Mother used to tell us that just before her marriage she had anticipated that once married to a brilliant rabbi she would, of course, be taught by him and become something so much more than the housekeeper and nursemaid that most wives were content to be. But my father was disconcerted with my mother's vision of herself and by her ambition to pursue her artistic and intellectual life after marriage; with the best will in the world and with all the affection in the world he remained puzzled by the frustration which occasionally rose up in her and found vent in some unexpected word or action. He was proud of his wife's accomplishments, but his view of a wife was essentially the old-fashioned Jewish one of the "woman of worth" and he never really appreciated what my mother had given up on marriage.

All this I saw, or thought I saw, and I would lie in bed at night mentally putting each one's case to the other—"But don't you *see* . . ." I suppose it is uncommon for a child of fifteen or so to feel in some respects paternal toward his parents, especially when one of the parents is at the same time a symbol of strength and dignity, but to me it was a characteristic feeling and colored my childhood from early adolescence. Walking with my father to the synagogue on a Saturday morning I would search my mind for something to say which I felt would encourage him. I reported to him anything flattering that my schoolmasters had said, not by way of boasting but to make him feel happy about me, and on a few occasions I made up things to tell him which I thought would help him to remain convinced that the world was going as he believed and wanted it to go. Similarly, when I came into the kitchen and found my mother occupied with some domestic task there, I would try to find something to say that would please and cheer her. This was more difficult, for my mother was (or seemed to me) an emotionally more complicated person. To my father, I thought that anything I could say which indicated that a world of enlightened moral idealism was showing increased respect for the Jewish people and their religion, or that people I had met had read and approved something he had written, or that I myself was developing so as eventually to play my part with dignity and credit in the Anglo-Jewish or Scottish-Jewish world—anything of this sort would please and cheer him (as I am sure it did). But to find the properly cheering words for my mother was a more difficult business, and in talking with her I often ended by displaying my own problems, something I do not remember once doing with my father.

This may help to explain why I considered my winning a school bursary in the summer of 1927 as something that was significant largely as a contribution to my parents' happiness. It is possible that I exaggerated the importance they attached to scholastic achievement and that I was attributing to them an attitude which I had partly absorbed from the competitive atmosphere of school itself and partly deduced from my father's own career and character as well as from the traditional Jewish (and, for that matter, also Scottish) attitude toward academic success; but there can at least be no doubt of the financial relief it must have been to my father to be saved from having to pay even the relatively small fees they charged at Watson's. After 1927 I won a bursary annually, and in my last year at school won a scholarship that carried me through Edinburgh University, so that henceforth my education did not cost my father anything. The fact that I was contributing to lessening the financial strain under which he continually labored gave me great satisfaction.

Life was fairly hard during my last four years at school. We had a considerable amount of homework to do, which was supposed to take about two hours but often (if I was wrestling with a complicated mathematical exercise, for example) took longer. Then, I was taking both piano and (after 1926) violin lessons, which involved practicing daily.

Of course I skimped my practicing, and often did little more than look over the week's assignment the day before my lesson, but still, having practicing as one of the things down on the list to be done, I could not feel free of an evening if I had not done it. We were supposed to do some Hebrew daily as well, as a rule prepare a piece of Biblical translation in which my father examined Lionel and me on Friday nights. Sometimes in the summer term I would be able to do my homework, my practicing of both piano and violin, and my Hebrew in a reasonably short time and feel myself really free to spend the rest of the afternoon and the evening as I pleased. This, however, was so unusual that I still remember some of the occasions when it happened and recall the sense of freedom and self-righteousness with which I went out to play in the Meadows with all my day's work done. Generally I went around with a sense of duty undone, for I often left homework uncompleted and the piano and violin untouched.

I liked music and was anxious to become proficient, but I had a fatal facility which enabled me to improvise and "mess about" instead of learning the hard way, so that I never developed the skill I could and should have acquired. My piano teacher was an interesting and able woman, Miss Lucy Brown, who came to the house one afternoon a week to give me my lesson. Over the years we developed a real friendship, and often we would sit and talk about my ambitions for the future or the pleasures of the different seasons or music and poetry, or indeed anything at all. Miss Brown was one of those spinster music teachers, so common throughout the country, with real talent but not sufficient to enable them to become professional performers, who eke out a bare living by giving weekly lessons to school-children. Her life was a fairly grim struggle, and as she trotted wearily around from one pupil to another she must have found her profession profoundly disappointing. She had a tiny flat in Alva Street, at the West End, and one day when she had hurt her ankle and could not walk she asked me to come there for my lesson. When I arrived I found that, having just washed her hair, she had it loose behind her back, and looked young and pretty. For the first time I realized that Miss Brown was a woman, and not merely a music teacher with some interesting ideas. Her old upright piano was in poor shape, and she apologized for it. Her flat was shabby and showed clearly the hardness of her struggle. I went away from that lesson (I was fifteen or sixteen at the time) seeing Miss Brown as a tragic, romantic figure, a beautiful and talented woman beaten down by harsh circumstances and facing a future of loneliness and poverty.

When I left school I continued with the violin but, realizing that I would not have the time to work at two instruments any longer, I gave up taking piano lessons. Miss Brown and I parted with reluctance. I think she was genuinely fond of me and had hoped that our weekly talks would continue. I thought of her often during my university years. In my final year at the university one of my fellow students told me that he wanted to begin taking piano lessons and I gave him Miss Brown's name and address. He wrote to her and he told me the following week that his letter had been returned marked "Deceased." Miss Brown, as I discovered later, had been suffering from a fatal malady when I had taken my farewell of her, though of course I knew nothing of it at the time.

When I think of Miss Brown now I think of our drawing room at Millerfield Place where I would have my lesson at 4:30 on Monday afternoons. The drawing room was not often used during the week. On Sunday afternoons in the winter a fire was lit there, and we generally had a family evening with music. Otherwise it was left unheated except for a small electric heater which was switched on whenever any one went up to practice. (I say "went up" because the drawing room was upstairs, on the first floor.) It was a large, fairly handsome room, with a white marble (or imitation marble? I always thought of it as marble) fireplace, some Constable reproductions on the walls, and in one corner the old Ernst Kapps grand piano that my father had bought second hand for my mother on their honeymoon for £9. Lionel or Sylvia would bring Miss Brown up a cup of tea soon after she arrived, and she would sit sipping it beside the piano while I went through my scales and arpeggios. My father, who generally took a nap from about three o'clock until half-past four, would often leave his stiff white artificial cuffs standing on a little table in the drawing room, and then come in to collect them when Miss Brown was there, forgetting that this was Monday and she would be giving me my lesson. He knew I was there, of course, by the sound of the piano, but thought I was just practicing. He would get up from his rest and refresh himself by washing his face in cold water (he always washed with a great deal of splashing and spluttering). Then he would barge into the drawing room (which was next to the bathroom) to collect his cuffs, breathing heavily after his cold-water wash. He would be well inside the room before he noticed Miss Brown, and the sight would cover him with confusion. He would mutter an apology, hastily seize the cuffs, and withdraw. This happened time and time again—the situation on each occasion repeating itself exactly—and every time I was equally embarrassed for my father.

I have talked about the development of my literary ambitions which I associate with the summer of 1927 and the solitary walking and brooding that I indulged in at that time. I remember one Monday evening about this time, after I had been playing for Miss Brown a piece by Frank Bridge whose name I forget but whose opening cadences I can still remember: I liked the piece, and played it well, and the music was running through my head as I leaned out of my bedroom window and listened to the sounds of Edinburgh coming up from the streets below—housewives beating carpets in the back greens of Livingstone Place, boys playing cricket in the Meadows, and the distant sound of bagpipes from the East Meadows, where public concerts were provided by the Corporation. Gradually the strains of the distant pipe music ousted the piano music from my consciousness, and I listened, unspeakably moved. I found the sound of bagpipes deeply rousing; it awakened my sense of Scottish history with its violence and its pageantry and its fatal predeliction for the lost cause. As I grew up Scotland became for me more and more an emotion rather than a country, and I would surrender myself to the emotion with a pleasing melancholy.

But of course I was Jewish, and my ancestors had no part in this romantic history: theirs had been a darker and more glorious destiny. My pride in Jewish history and my feeling for its particular kind of sadness existed side by side with my attitude to Scotland. It was largely a matter of mood (how much, in my childhood, was largely a matter of mood!). The Scottish mood rose to the sound of the bagpipes or the sight of Edinburgh Castle fading in the purple darkness; the Jewish mood came with the elegiac synagogue chants and the plaintive melodies of Jewish liturgy and folk song. Each mood excluded the other: in the Scottish mood the Jewish world seemed distant and unimportant,

[76]

and in the Jewish mood Scottish history and traditions seemed modern and shabby. It was now that I became acutely aware of living in two worlds, or rather of moving freely between one and the other. Bagpipe music and synagogue melody represented the two poles between which my sensibility moved. I accepted this dualism as part of the nature of things, and looking back now I wonder at the ease which which I did so.

My last year at school—1929 to 1930—was my happiest and most fruitful. Having passed my Higher Leaving Certificate the year before in all the necessary subjects, including mathematics, physics, and chemistry, I was now free to drop the subjects in which I was less interested and less able and concentrate on English, history, Latin, and Greek. This year was a kind of interregnum between school and university, with something of the best points of each. The classes were small and the subjects were congenial. One got to know the masters, who appeared at last as helpful human beings rather than merely as teachers. I worked hard, writing extra Latin prose because the Latin master had interested me in the possibility of imitating different kinds of Latin prose style. I read an immense amount outside the regular schoolwork, taking out from the Carnegie Library the works of Ibsen and Strindberg and Bjornson as well as Galsworthy, Shaw, and Conrad; I read—and resented—Spengler's *Decline of the West;* I took the poems of Keats and Spenser with me on walks to Blackford Hill; I rolled Homer's Greek on my tongue and thought with pity and almost with contempt of those who were unable to do likewise. I even, in a very small way, became a leader in a school activity, for I played the violin in the school orchestra and was now made its leader. I contributed to the *Watsonian* a verse translation of a chorus from Euripides' *Medea* and of a poem by Alfred de Vigny. And at the end of a year pulsing with literary ambition and self-confidence I won a scholarship to the university and enough prizes to satisfy even my view of what my father would wish for me.

On prize-giving day, as I staggered off the platform balancing some £20 worth of books (representing special prizes in English, Latin, Greek, history, and essay-writing), I thought of my father sitting among the parents and being at last really proud of his son. He shook hands with me afterward and said "Well done!"—something he had never done before, for he was a shy man who could not easily speak words of praise to those close to him. Later, at the woodwork exhibition held in the school's art room, I watched him maneuver his way into the vicinity of the headmaster and his deputy and overheard him thanking them, in a courtly little speech, for all they had done for me. As a matter of fact, neither of those particular individuals had done anything for me; but they stood for those who had, and my father's act was symbolic. It set a seal on my school career. I looked across at my father and was proud of his pride in me; I felt that I had done something, had helped to increase his dignity and vindicate the character of the Jew in Scotland. I had not let him down. Walking home across the Meadows with my parents, carrying my heavy load of prize books, I felt that I had no more to ask of life. The July sun was shining; ahead lay the summer holidays; and in the autumn the university and the promise of the free life of letters.

CHAPTER 4

I believe a schoolteacher wrote a book some years ago **with** the title *Friday Thank God*. That phrase expresses perfectly my attitude to the arrival of the week end during term time when I was a schoolboy. The daily grind of school, with its abundant homework, its fierce competition, the sense of never being able to relax, pressed heavily upon me, in spite of the fact that I often enjoyed the actual classroom work. Waking up in the morning with the knowledge that one simply had to get out of bed, that there was no possibility of turning over for an extra doze, and seeing the hours of school stretching ahead, was a dismal experience, especially on a Monday. We had a maid once who would climb each morning with grim steps up to the attic floor where Lionel and I slept in one bedroom and my sister Sylvia in another, and announce in deep, funereal tones: "Lionel, David, Sylvia—time!" I used to lie waiting for that ominous tread on the uncarpeted attic stairs (they were covered with a flower-patterned yellow linoleum), and the voice it heralded sounded in my ears like a summons to damnation. The anticipation was always worse than the reality; I don't remember ever being especially unhappy in class; but the oppressive weight of the knowledge of a full day's school ahead remained a characteristic sensation of my childhood and disappeared only after I had left school and entered the university, where the smaller number of classes to be attended and the freedom of the student to come and go meant a completely new kind of academic world. To wake up on a Thursday morning was to feel the end of the week already lying ahead, and Friday morning was positively rose-colored. The last "period" (as each of our lessons was called) on a Friday, whatever the subject, had its special happy flavor of the end of the week, and one walked home from school on a Friday afternoon (however much homework had been assigned for the Monday) with the tread of an escaped prisoner. Friday night, with two solid days before school again, was the best night of the week; Saturday night, with still a whole day between it and Monday, was pleasant in a quite different way; Sunday night was full of the threat of Monday morning.

Sometimes there were unexpected respites—a half-holiday for the replay of a football match which some unforeseen circumstance had caused to be cancelled the preceding Saturday, or the sudden dismissal of school an hour or two before the usual time because of some unexpected crisis or celebration. But these respites were few and far between. Once a term we had the annual mid-term holiday, a Monday off, which made a luxuriously long week end (but it seemed to go just as fast as ordinary week ends), and occasionally in winter if there had been a continuous hard frost for some days we would get a whole day's "skating holiday." These were blessed breaks in routine, but not, of course, comparable to the holidays we got at Christmas and at Easter—three weeks each in my earlier schooldays, later tragically reduced to a fortnight, and then (if my recollection of loss is not misleading me) to a mere ten days. But "the" holidays were the summer holidays, the two months' vacation we got in the summertime, and it was these months toward which the whole year moved.

There were three phases of the summer holidays. First the week or two at the end of the summer term, when the year's marks were already in (so that nothing that one did *counted*) yet classes still went on. There was a wonderful sense of relaxation about those days. The unrelenting competition in marks which had gone on throughout the school year suddenly ceased, for the prizes and scholarships were now allotted; masters unbent, and not only amused us with Latin crosswords or intriguing stunts in the science laboratories, but would chat in human and friendly fashion about climbing and fishing. I remember once, at this time of the year, "Billie" Williams, our mathematics master, sat down unexpectedly on the bench beside me and began to give me advice on trout fishing, going into such practical details as the price of rods and telling me where I could get a cheap but serviceable one. This period between the end of the examinations and the prize-giving (with which the school session formally concluded) was in some respects the best part of all the year, for the other two parts of summer were lying happily ahead—the month at the seaside, and the further month of freedom in Edinburgh before school started again.

Pure bliss seemed to stretch endlessly on the horizon. Two months seemed a long, long time in those days; indeed, I used to have the feeling that for all practical purposes I could look forward to a period of permanent felicity. I would walk home across the Meadows in the July sunshine, wearing my summer school clothes of gray

cricket shirt, gray shorts, and red Watson's blazer, and
savor my happiness with conscious relish. I could hardly
believe that three strenuous school terms had indeed rolled
away and the longed-for, dreamed-of, almost (it seemed at
times) mythical summer holidays were at hand, unspoiled
as yet, lying intact and promising just ahead. It all seemed
too good to be true. Wishes didn't come true in this life—
I knew that: all my early childhood I longed desperately
for a tricycle, which my parents could never afford, and
later the wish was transferred to a bicycle, and there, too,
I was permanently disappointed. (I bought my first bicycle
for myself when I was twenty-one, with prize money I had
won at Edinburgh University.) How often had I stood outside sweet shops with empty pockets longing for a penny
or two to materialize somehow, or hung on the outskirts
of a crowd around an ice-cream barrow wondering whether
the ice-cream man would be miraculously inspired to offer
me a "cornet" or a "slider" free. These things never happened. (The few pence a week pocket money we received
was to be put into a money box and saved, and during our
early childhood Lionel, Sylvia, and I never had anything
to spend for ourselves.) Yet summer and the summer holidays did come; the school year did come to an end; and
one did find oneself at last standing by the trunks and suitcases outside No. 6, Millerfield Place, waiting for the taxi
(glorious vehicle) that was to convey the family and its
luggage to the railway station.

It had been horse cabs when I was very young, but the
taxi soon established itself in my gallery of exciting and
anticipated objects, and the very smell of its exhaust set
the heart beating faster. The leathery smell inside, the
straps hanging down from the adjustable, rattling windows,
the little folding seats that could be pulled out for us

[82]

children to sit on—how thoroughly delectable these things were! And then to watch as the taxi came into the precincts of the station, marked by the appearance of hoardings covered with advertising posters—Stephen's ink, Oxo, Bovril, Virol ("growing girls need it"), Pear's soap, the Pickwick, the Owl and the Waverly pen, that come as a Boon and a Blessing to men. These were signposts to adventure, indications that we were nearing the actual station, with its infinite glories. People have complained of the typical British railway station, with its noise, its dirt, its apparent confusion; but as a child I found it magnificently thrilling (an attitude I have never wholly lost). Porters rushing about with barrows heaped with luggage, the noise of trains arriving and departing, carriage doors slamming, the guard blowing his whistle, engines letting off steam, uniformed boys with trays strapped to their chests shouting "Chocolates! Cigarettes!," trolleys with newspapers and confectionery being wheeled along the platform, everywhere the sense of movement, bustle, excitement, and romance. And to know that one was going off oneself in a train, out beyond Haymarket tunnel, across the Forth Bridge, beyond, beyond—such knowledge made the railway station the most perfect spot on earth. Waverley Station, Edinburgh, was an especially good station; it was large, busy, noisy, with a great number of platforms and trains departing for almost every possible direction.

On these occasions my father always wore an air of businesslike efficiency. I had watched him write out and tie on the labels, heard him ring up for the taxi, observed his supervision of the taxi driver as he stowed the luggage in the taxi (always a difficult job, for our family traveled with mountains of luggage), accompanied him to one of the station bookstalls where he methodically bought papers

[83]

to read in the train—a *Scotsman* for himself, a *Bulletin,* perhaps, for my mother, and a *Children's Newspaper* or sometimes even (for we were on holiday) an illustrated magazine or two for us children. And now as he collected his family round him at the barrier and presented the tickets, he was very much the paterfamilias leading a family expedition. He would personally see that the heavy luggage was safely stowed in the luggage van, waving his stick at porters and directing them in tones of firm authority that only occasionally gave way to accents of urgency and even anxiety. But at last we were settled in the compartment, the hand luggage stowed safely on the luggage rack, the corner seats argued over and finally allocated—there being five of us and a compartment, of course, having only four corners. The atmosphere of tension and hurry which had surrounded all our movements suddenly relaxed; we were early after all; and there was plenty of time before the train moved off.

Sitting in the train, waiting for the guard's whistle to announce to the engine driver that it was time for him to start, I would revel in anticipation. And when the train began slowly to move, passing the porters and their barrows as they stood on the platform, passing the bookstall, the advertisements on the wall, moving out into the open past the hissing engines of stationary trains, the real adventure began. Through the deep cutting that traversed Princess Street Gardens at the base of the Castle Rock, then into the dark of Haymarket tunnel, a brief stop at Haymarket station, and out past the western suburbs of Edinburgh to the open fields that lay between the city and South Queensferry, where the Forth Bridge began. As the train rumbled across the Forth Bridge we three children all crowded to the window to look down on the Forth lying like a river on a map hundreds of feet below. The water lapping the shores, the ships looking like toys yet at the same time excitingly real, the whole sense of living geography that came over me as I looked down from the moving train, made me feel strangely as though I were both viewing and participating in the grand rolling of the earth in its relentless diurnal movement. I felt curiously moved. Years later, I discovered that precisely this emotion was brought back on reading the lines of Keats:

> The moving waters at their priestlike task
> Of pure ablution round earth's human shores.

It was something to do with a sense of the steady way in which the world of geography carried on unperturbed by the petty daily affairs of men in cities, and I recaptured it vividly not long ago when watching the waves break on a deserted beach at night.

In 1920 we spent August in Kilrenny, a tiny village a mile away from the Fife fishing town of Anstruther. This was the first of many holidays spent on the shores of Fife— at St. Andrews, at Leven (twice), and for seven successive years at Crail. But the 1920 holiday was especially exciting, for it was the first time the family had gone off for a month's holiday since we had settled in Edinburgh. In 1919, because of my mother's illness and presumably also because the move to Edinburgh had meant enough travel (and expense) for one year, we did not go away at all. In earlier years we had spent our holidays either with my paternal grandparents in Leeds or with my mother's people in Liverpool. This time we were going away to the seaside, like so many other middle-class people, and my joy in the adventure was increased by the knowledge that we were behaving as a family should.

[85]

The house we were bound for was one of a group of three which stood together at the edge of a common and which, apart from a few farmhouses and a cottage or two, constituted the entire village of Kilrenny. My father had learned of it through an advertisement in the Edinburgh daily paper, the *Scotsman*. The description of the house in the advertisement had sounded suitable, and the rent was reasonable, so my father wrote off to the owner (an elderly spinster by the name of Miss Gardner) to ask for further particulars. Miss Gardner's reply arrived one afternoon in July, soon after I had come home from school. I was lying lazily on the dining-room sofa, and Mother was sitting in an armchair in a corner of the room, when my father entered with a letter in his hand. I remember him standing in the recess by the bay window reading out the letter to my mother. As he read, it dawned upon me that this was a description of the house where we might be going for our holidays, and I listened intently. I have a vivid recollection of my father reading out, in a somewhat singsong tone, the phrase ". . . and it has a W.C. . . . ," emphasizing rythmically the first, third, and fifth syllables, and giving an approving nod of his head. I knew at that moment that he would take the house. And I said to myself: *"As long as I live, I shall never forget Daddy standing there by the window reading out those words: 'and it has a W.C.'"*

Having crossed the Forth Bridge, the train wound up the Fife coast, every now and again coming right out onto the sea, running by villages, harbors, golf courses, beaches, stretches of rocks and shingle. One caught fascinating glimpses of a calm sea rippling up a sandy cove, a patch of seaweed covered rocks, children playing on a beach, a golfer bending down to put his ball on the tee. Aberdour;

[86]

Burntisland, where one caught a glimpse of fairly large freight vessels in the harbor; a stretch of bright red sand which seemed to be a deposit from an aluminum factory (this is what I believed as a child; I have not the remotest idea whether this is the true explanation of the red sand or indeed of what an aluminum factory is); Kirkaldy, where the smell of linoleum floated strongly in, from the factories of Barrie, Ostlere, and Shepherd; Dysart; Thornton Junction, where the line swerved inland; back to the coast again at Leven; a brief stop at the tiny station of Lundin Links; the picturesque fishing villages and holiday resorts of Largo, Elie, St. Monans, and Pittenweem; and finally Anstruther, the nearest station to Kilrenny. Miss Gardner had arranged to have a car meet us, and we bundled in and were driven to the house. It had that half musty, cottagey smell that all country houses seem to have, and I took that as a guarantee of its authenticity, proof that we were well away from the city. It was, in fact, a thrilling smell. I discovered that I was to share an attic bedroom with my brother Lionel. The evening light was coming in at the window when I first saw it, and it looked golden and old-fashioned and rustic and peaceful.

Lionel, Sylvia, and I were up early the next morning, and we had explored the common before breakfast. There was a burn running through it, which was very satisfactory; there were also some local small boys who shouted derisive remarks at us, which was less pleasing. After breakfast, Mother chased us all (including my father) out of the house, while she unpacked. My father decided that we ought to find out the way to the sea. He appeared dressed for the expedition. He had discarded the black frock coat he wore almost always in Edinburgh (except on very hot days, when he would wear, at home, a black alpaca jacket) and wore instead a dark gray lounge suit. He still wore his black bow tie and his stiff collar, but the stiff artificial shirt front was gone, and so were the stiff cuffs. On his head he had neither the glossy silk hat he wore in Edinburgh on all occasions of even the slightest formality, nor the broad-brimmed black soft hat he used in the city while out on more ordinary business, but a cloth "traveling cap" of a brownish-gray color. He wore a dark gray topcoat and carried a stout walking stick. On future holidays his old-fashioned formality of attire was to diminish much further, under the pressure of his children's criticism and a general change in the atmosphere of the times; in Crail in the early 1930's he wore a blue blazer and gray flannel trousers with a gray sweater and a cricket shirt with a light gray tie; but in 1920 he had not yet learned to relax so completely. Earnest idealist that he was, he felt it necessary to carry around with him, even on holiday, some indication of his responsibilities as representative of and spokesman for the Jewish way of life before the clergy and laity of Scotland. He was forty years old then.

We discovered that it was quite a long walk to the sea, and to get to the shingly beach we had to pass through the adjacent village of Cellardyke. It astonished us that in less than a mile we should have moved from one village to another, but it added to the sense of adventure and exploration. At Cellardyke we discovered a small grocer's and confectioner's shop, and my father, announcing that he would buy some sweets, marshaled us all in. He inquired of the proprietor (Mr. Allan, I think his name was) with grave courtesy what kind of chocolates he had in stock, and Mr. Allan brought out samples of different kinds and laid them on the counter. "Very good these," he said, of one variety. "Try one." And to our astonishment he popped one briskly into my father's mouth. My father chewed the chocolate meditatively, then nodded, and, with an almost ritual solemnity, proceeded to purchase half a pound. Mr. Allan then directed us to the beach, where we spent the rest of the morning.

Spending a considerable part of every day by the beach was a ritual with us when on holiday. We came for the sea air, and nothing was going to prevent us from getting it. I don't remember bad weather ever keeping us indoors: rain or shine we were in the fresh air absorbing health. My father in particular would waste no second of his precious holiday. I have known him to sit outside for hours in the pouring rain, holding an umbrella over his head as he gazed meditatively out to sea. At the end of the month, sun, wind, and rain had always weathered his face to a rich brown, and when the Jewish High Festivals came, as they often did, early in September, my father's weather-beaten face would look quite startling as he stood in the pulpit in his white kittel.

My mother got out less often; she had the house to run, and she was left to cook the meals and wash the dishes while the rest of the family sought the open air. Sometimes we had a maid with us on holiday, sometimes we hadn't (we had none in Kilrenny), but in either case my mother had much to do in the house, and never really had a proper holiday. She would join us at the beach after we had been there for an hour or two, and leave early to prepare the next meal. She did go bathing with us however (sea bathing was another daily ritual in our family when on holiday) and it was she who taught us all to swim, including my father. Heroically determined, he learned to swim at the age of forty, and though he never swam well, he swam conscientiously, and always stayed in the water much longer than any of the rest of us. His technique of bathing was all his own. He would walk into the sea up to his waist, and then bob right down until the sea covered his head, two or three times in rapid succession. Then he would act as though he were washing his face with sea water. And after that he would swim a short distance with short, rapid strokes, before standing up and repeating the ducking performance. Mother would swim gracefully about for a while and then take each of us children out to deepish water and, holding us up by the chin, give us a swimming lesson. Then she would warm herself up by a further swim before coming out. I may be wrong, but my impression is that my father wore the same bathing costume (our family always stuck to that good old Victorian term) all the years I knew him; it started off by being a very dark blue, but after some years it became a faded light blue in color and also got pretty tattered and frayed about the edges. Some time about 1930 my mother bought him a rainbow-colored beach robe, of which he grew very fond. He would wear it down to the water's edge, where he would discard it while he went into the water, and then put it on as soon as he came out. I can see him now, panting and dripping, with the water streaming down from his graying hair, as he struggles into his rainbow robe.

Swimming was not the only sport that my father took up relatively late in life. In 1922 we spent our summer holiday in Leven, a Fife town of some respectable size, beside the coal port of Methil. Leven, though far from being as quiet and rustic as Kilrenny, had a large and excellent beach and it also had several first-rate golf courses. It was here, on the comparatively easy "ladies' course," that Lionel and I first played golf, and it was here, too, that my father first played the royal and ancient game. The three of us started off with three clubs among us—a driver, a cleek, and a putter—and no instruction of any kind. We simply imitated what we deemed to be the movements of other golfers. My father, who was a small man of robust physique but with relatively poor physical co-ordination, would address the ball with a swift, desperate, jerking movement; it never occurred to him that he might have a better chance of hitting it if he took a slow backswing. After pondering the ball for a moment he would jerk his club back a few feet and then, without any pause at all, jerk it forward to the ball. He would miss, or top or slice the ball more often than not, but sometimes, by sheer good luck, would land it a smart crack which would send it a fair distance. His gratification at such a lucky shot was immense. I believe he thought that all success in such physical activities was due entirely to good luck, and he had no awareness of how impossibly bad his golf was. He had the hands of a writer and scholar, with stubby fingers which looked most at home when curved about a pen. He was quite handy about the house in such things as mending fuses, and he fancied himself as a watchmaker and would pick away at a broken watch with a pin until he had rendered it beyond repair, but he was hopeless at anything that required delicacy of physical co-ordination. He was occasionally taken out fishing by a wealthy member of his congregation who had taken up the sports of the landed gentry, and on one occasion he caught the back of his coat with his very first cast. He was regarded as dangerous with a fishing rod, but not to the fish. He had great stamina, however, and until fairly late in life would walk for miles without fatigue.

My father, Lionel, and I playing golf together were, I suppose, something of a symbol of the attitude of the

Daiches family to sport. With one set of three clubs among the three of us, we would pass the clubs around as needed, often to the amazement and sometimes to the annoyance of golfers coming up behind us. Often I would dash fifty yards, to where my father was, to hand him the cleek after I had used it myself, while Lionel, who could not be bothered to go and fetch it after my father had used it, would make his slow progress down the fairway with a putter. We would lose balls frequently too; my father's propensity to wild slicing often resulting in the disappearance of the ball into a clump of whin bushes after his drive. Once we played with one ball as well as only three clubs, taking alternate shots. This was at the very beginning of our golfing careers. The next year we acquired a mashie and a jigger, and a little later my father discovered that a putting green was really more his style. He became fairly efficient as a putter, and would often invite Lionel or me to what he called "a game of putt." Lionel and I continued to play, on the Balcomie golf course at Crail, with one set of clubs between us. Eventually Lionel gave up golf altogether and I inherited the five family clubs, two of which I replaced with new ones bought at Thornton's, in Edinburgh, with bursary money. I played occasionally with schoolmates on the Braid Hills course, and continued to play sporadically during my university days. I was never very good, but did acquire a modest competence at the game. I never had more than six clubs, and gave up the game completely when it became the fashion for golfers to carry a whole armory of weapons around with them on the golf course. When I see golfers today going off to play with their enormous array of clubs, I think of the old men of Edinburgh in the 1920's who would go round the ancient and modest little course at Bruntsfield with a single club and then walk slowly home in the summer dusk, with the club held horizontally by the middle of the shaft, swinging to and fro as the arms swung.

I think it was on our summer holidays in Fife that my father first learned to relax. His earlier life had been intellectually strenuous, intense, dedicated. To become over a period of a few years both an authority on David Hume and an orthodox rabbi thoroughly grounded in the enormous complexities of Talmudic theory and practice was a remarkable feat, and can have left no time for relaxation of any kind. And then, as a young minister in Hull and later in Sunderland, fired with the passionate ideal of a living Judaism domiciled happily in an English cultural context, preaching, lecturing, exhorting, pleading, before apathetic audiences in shabby synagogues and meeting places, belligerently optimistic, positively messianic in his visionary hopes, yet grimly realistic in his appraisal of the material he had to work with—it was an exhausting life, with no room anywhere for triviality. When he settled in Edinburgh in March, 1919, to become rabbi of the Edinburgh Hebrew Congregation and virtual spiritual head of the Jews in Scotland, he soon made emotional contact, as it were, with eighteenth-century Edinburgh (he was already familiar with it intellectually) and developed a Scottish-Jewish ideal that increased its hold on him with the years. And it was on his seaside holidays in Scotland that he learned to relax.

It did not happen all at once. Each year he shed more of his formal clothing when on holiday and became more successful in temporarily laying aside his official personality. At Crail in the late 1920's and early 1930's the process went on apace, and when, after my final year at Edinburgh University, the family went to the North West Highlands for August, my father had acquired (but of course for holiday use only) something of the air and apparel of a sporting country gentleman. And while in earlier years he had taken away with him for holiday reading some heavy philosophical or theological volume, I once found him in the summer of 1934 reading a paper-bound French novel.

His smoking habits changed too, and this affected more than his holiday practice. My father was a connoisseur of Havana cigars, and for years would smoke nothing else— which meant that he generally smoked nothing at all, for he could rarely afford Havana cigars and depended largely on presents of cigars he received occasionally from more well-to-do members of his congregation (who were, incidentally, few in number: the Jews of Edinburgh in those days were not on the whole a prosperous lot). He would save a few Havana cigars to smoke on his holiday. But once—it was at Leven, I think, in 1922—not having any Havana cigars and not being able to afford to buy any, he decided to try cigarettes for the first time in his life— not ordinary cigarettes, of course, but Russian cigarettes, which somehow had more dignity than the vulgar variety and at the same time tasted perhaps a little more like a Havana cigar. But they were unsatisfactory. My father puffed at them in the clumsy way in which a cigar smoker will smoke a cigarette, and he was manifestly unsatisfied. For the next few years it was again Havana cigars or nothing. And then, about 1930, he was persuaded to try a pipe as a holiday smoke. A member of his congregation presented him with a curved-stem pipe and half a pound of Balkan Sobranie, the richest and most cigarlike of tobaccos. From that time on, he was a regular pipe smoker, always smoking Balkan Sobranie tobacco and always using a pipe with a curved stem. Of course, he still smoked Havana cigars when he could get them, but during the day, not only on holiday but also at home when he sat working in his study, he would puff away at his pipe. He was not a skillful pipe smoker, and he would allow moisture to accumulate in his pipe so that his puffing often produced an audible bubbling.

I remember once, when Lionel and I were in our early twenties and had been for some years pipe smokers ourselves, finding one of our father's pipes on the dining-room mantelpiece and discovering that it had become so carbonized that the hollow in the bowl was only about a quarter of an inch in diameter. Much amused, we pointed this out to our father, who smiled shyly and said that he had noticed that the pipe seemed to have been getting smaller but he had never been quite sure why. Either Lionel or I—I cannot remember which of us, now—scraped out the bowl for him and he received the restored pipe with gratitude and delight.

We first went to Crail in 1927, and went there for seven successive summers, generally, though not always, to the same house. This little Fife town thus takes a special place in my recollection of childhood summers. It was— and is—an unpretentious but picturesque town on the sea almost at the eastern extremity of Fife, the East Neuk of Fife as it is called. There was an old stone harbor at one end of the town, a pleasant but small beach at the other, and a great variety of rocks and rock pools between. Our time would be divided between the beach, from which we bathed daily (except Saturdays) and the rocks, where Lionel and I would spend hour after hour watching the marine life and catching the "grannies" and other fish that inhabited the pools. Sometimes we would go for walks, to

[95]

Anstruther, four miles away, or to St. Andrews, ten miles in the opposite direction, or, more frequently, to the big beach at Balcomie, round at the other side of Fife Ness, where the sand was lighter and finer than the sand at Crail. There was a confectioner's, known as Mrs. Aird's, where the young people would gather of an evening to buy ice cream or fish and chips, but our family was seldom there. True, we all had an ice cream a day, after bathing: that was a ritual, and the ice cream was bought from a stand by the beach. (It strikes me with amazement now that we should have wanted to eat ice cream after bathing in the chill waters of the North Sea.) But, quite apart from the fact that Mrs. Aird's fish and chips would not have been kosher, having been fried in animal fat, we did not mingle with the "fast" set that frequented such haunts: our holiday was open air and active and innocent. We swam, walked, fished, played on the sand, occasionally played golf on the Balcomie golf course, or sat reading by the sea.

Toward the end of August, as the evenings began to draw in, we would walk in the dusk along the Castle Walk, a picturesque path which began round the corner from our house and ran along the top of a field which sloped down to the rocks and the sea. There were wooden benches placed at intervals along the Castle Walk, and there my father would often sit in wet weather or in the evening after dark. He made friends with a Mr. Greig, Church of Scotland minister from Airdrie, and they would sit side by side at night talking of the differences and similarities between their two religions while the fragrant aroma of Balkan Sobranie floated over the Castle Walk. Walking along there after dark, I could smell the tobacco and hear the murmur of voices before I could make out the figures on the bench, and the tobacco smell and the murmur of voices mingled with the plash of the sea below to produce a complex sensation which I still recall vividly to bring back my father in Crail in late August.

But Mrs. Aird's remained a disturbing and even a seductive image. These were the years of my adolescence, and the young men and women hanging around Mrs. Aird's stood for a world of sexual adventure whose very thought was absolutely incompatible with the atmosphere of our family life. As far as Lionel and I were able to discover, sex did not exist in the Daiches family. Neither of our parents ever addressed to us a single word about it, at any time. My father's notion, I think, was that one kept oneself pure by hard work and idealistic ambitions until one had completed one's professional training, and then a suitable bride was brought to one's attention, with whom one fell in love and in marriage to whom one's sex interests were first awakened. I found my own adolescence disturbing and embarrassing, and I thought the imaginations to which it gave rise were both unique and guilty. I suppose it is comic or even pathetic that a small confectioner's-cum-fish-and-chip shop in a little seaside town should have represented to me, and I think to Lionel as well, a world of forbidden desire. For years afterward the smell of fish and chips had a more erotic tang to me than perfumes named "Ecstasy" or "Desire," though by the time I was really grown up my taste had become more conventional in this respect.

August always went by too quickly, and all too soon we would find ourselves preparing for the return to Edinburgh. Preparations began a day or two before we actually left. There was an immense amount of packing to be done, which Mother undertook pretty well single-handed. For years we traveled with our own meat dishes (for we could not eat off the meat dishes of a non-Jewish house) and mother had supplies of meat sent out by post from the Edinburgh Jewish butcher. Packing a trunk full of dishes was an arduous business, and eventually Mother gave it up and we went vegetarian throughout August—which was no hardship, for Mother could do marvelous things with fish (the term vegetarian in our family meant simply eating no meat but did not exclude fish). Slowly and gradually, and I believe never consciously on my parents' part, we relaxed a bit in the matter of diet. When she was first married Mother baked all her own bread, but ceased to do this after her illness in 1919. And on holiday one found oneself going a little further than one would have done in the city. In Edinburgh, we usually ate bread from the Jewish bakery, but occasionally we would get a loaf from a non-Jewish shop. Cakes and biscuits we regularly got from non-Jewish sources. But though Mother would buy ordinary cakes from a non-Jewish baker, she would always make her own pastry, for pastry from a gentile shop was liable to have been made with lard. On holiday, however, pastries started to creep in among the cakes bought for tea, and nobody raised the question of what they were made with. "Squashed flies"—cakes made by squashing a mass of currants between two layers of pastry—were originally forbidden if not homemade, but squashed flies from an ordinary baker first found their way to our table when we were on holiday in St. Andrews. True, we never bathed on Saturdays or did anything on that day except sit and read on the beach or go for decorous walks; and we said our daily Hebrew prayers and read the weekly portion of the law in Crail as in Edinburgh; yet the strictness of reli-

[98]

gious observance was relaxed when we were away on holiday, slightly and by slow degrees, but definitely.

I have mentioned that my father unbent on holiday in a way he rarely did at home. During the last few years that the whole family took its holiday together—when I was a student at Edinburgh and a research student at Oxford—I was able, on holiday walks, to speak to him in a man-to-man way for the first time in my life. We had, of course, often argued together in a friendly way, but never really talked as though we were contemporaries and equals. But now he began to talk to Lionel and me as though he really wanted our opinion. He would even ask our advice on something he was writing or some course of action he was contemplating. By this time he had become very much part of the Scottish scene, a Scottish rabbi with the emphasis as much on the "Scottish" as on the "rabbi," devoted to the Scottish countryside, more and more regarding his Judaism as part of the Scottish milieu. I have a clear picture of him one Saturday morning in August, 1934, in a remote West Highland village, sitting on a rock looking out at the Hebrides, his old dog-eared *Chumesh* (Hebrew Pentateuch) open on his lap at that day's portion of the law. His head was covered, of course, because he was reading the Bible; but it was with a soft-brimmed hat, not a skullcap. And I remember the evening of the same day: we had stood on the shore watching the western sun go down with unusual splendor, and as we lingered there in the hushed Highland night I heard my father singing faintly to himself the old Hebrew song about Elijah the prophet returning to his people, one of the songs traditionally sung after the Sabbath had departed and comfort was required to face the workaday world again.

It was on this holiday, too, that we took an excursion on

[99]

one of the MacBrayne steamers to the Isle of Skye. The weather was dull, and rain threatened; Lionel and I slipped down to the ship's bar for a comfortable beer. We were seated in a corner drinking export ale when we both became aware simultaneously of our father sitting at the opposite corner of the bar with a glass of lager before him. I had never known him to enter a bar before, and never known him to drink beer, though he had done so, I knew, in his student days. He took his glass and came over to our table. "Hello," he said. "What are you doing here?" We laughed, and replied: "Same as you." He smiled, and seemed at a loss for words—shy, but not embarrassed. Finally, he said: "It's a funny thing: your beer is dark brown and mine is pale yellow."

That was in 1934. When I look back on holidays by the sea, however, it is my childhood in the 'twenties that I recall most frequently. Just as I remember so vividly the joy and excitement of setting out on holiday, so I remember the desperate desire to cling to the last moments before time had ticked them away and we had to leave for home. I used to stand on the beach and look around and say to myself: "I'm here now, at *this minute,* and nothing can take this minute away." But it went. Coming home from the holidays had its compensations, however. There was the train journey again, and train journeys were always exciting, in whatever direction one was going. And there were always things of our own that we had perforce left behind which we were glad to get back to. School was almost a month away still. As the evenings drew in and the return to school grew closer, the idea of winter grew attractively cosy. School itself—a new year, a new class, new books—had its attractive side, and I would promise myself that this year I would really master everything from the very first, never leave things to be swotted up in a rush before the exams but by steady work achieve an effortless mastery of every subject and end the year covered with scholarships and prizes and glory. This resolution generally lasted about a week after the opening of term, but it was wonderfully sustaining while it did last.

How large our house in Millerfield Place looked when we first came back to it after our holiday! How high the ceilings were, yet how shut in the house was, with other houses staring at us from across the street. "Yesterday at this time I was swimming in the sea"; "a week ago today we went for a walk to St. Andrews." Slowly we ceased to dwell on our past holiday and surrendered to the different excitement of autumn. There was a briskness in the September air that moved one's thoughts to the future. My father had resumed his frock coat and formality of manner and was busy preparing for the High Festivals. How right, I used to feel, was the Jewish tradition of having the New Year in September! Everything was beginning afresh, a new working year was setting in, a chance to do bigger and better things than ever before. The year began with the retreat from out of doors, with the drawing of curtains and the poking up of the fire, the re-establishment of the claims of the domestic interior. In the gardens of the quiet streets of South Edinburgh they were burning dead leaves, and the smell of the burning leaves was for me the sad-sweet dirge of the outdoor life, of the life of sand and sea and field, and at the same time the heady promise of—of what? Of something better, anyway, something exciting, something really worthwhile, something I could achieve myself by an effort of the will. Yes, I could and I would: this year I would show them!

CHAPTER 5

I always found it next to impossible to imagine my father as a child. This was not only because, as a rabbi and a well-known public figure in Edinburgh, he had a dignity and formality of manner infinitely removed from the world of childhood, but also because I knew nothing of the circumstances of his childhood and thus found it impossible to visualize them. I am not even sure where or when he was born. The date of his birth he usually gave as 1880, but his birth certificate was dated March 10, 1881. He had some story of the records of the town in Poland where he was born having been destroyed by fire, and new birth certificates issued later to replace those which had been burned: the issuing clerk evidently drew on his memory for the details, and got the date of my father's birth wrong by a year. My father himself seemed somewhat vague about the story; but he always maintained that his true date of birth was 1880, in spite of his birth certificate. His insurance company, however, insisted on believing the birth certificate, and that was to his advantage as far as life insurance premiums were concerned. Exactly where in Poland he was born I am not certain: at one time I thought Vilna was the place, and on other occasions my father would mention the village of Neustadt (Neistodt in Yiddish pronunciation) as though it were his birthplace. My impression is that he was born in Vilna but, his father moving soon after to Neustadt, he spent his early childhood in the latter town. Poland was then, of course, under Russian rule. Vilna is, I believe, historically as much Lithuanian as Polish, but I think my father thought of it as Polish.

One of the reasons for my vagueness about these details is that my father disliked talking about them. I don't think he made more than half a dozen references to his childhood during all the years that I knew him. He was the second son of a distinguished rabbi and scholar, and scion of a long line of rabbis and scholars which stretched back to the early Middle Ages. From all I can gather, his infancy was spent in strenuous Jewish and Hebrew scholarship: I remember he once referred to his studying Talmud as a small boy by the light of rush candles stuck in the wall. This suggests poverty as well as precocity, yet I don't think the family were poor, for I believe my grandmother brought with her a reasonable dowry and for some time her father supported my grandfather while he lived a life of pure scholarship and meditation. My father once told a story of a "nurse" putting her head out of the window and shrieking out that a pig had got into the courtyard, to which he (then a very small boy) impertinently replied that he had seen no pig before the nurse appeared at the window. A nurse and a courtyard suggest some degree of prosperity. However that may be, my grandfather sent his sons to high school across the German border, in Koenigsberg, where my father attended the Gymnasium and acquired a sound education in the classics. The only other fact I remember hearing about my father's childhood is that his parents did not make a party for him at the celebration of his *bar mitzvah* (confirmation, at the age of thirteen), as is the usual custom: the reason for this was that his elder brother, my Uncle Samuel, had made himself so sick with overeating at the party held in celebration of *his bar mitzvah* that my grandparents thought it safer to omit that part of the proceedings when my father's turn came. My Uncle Samuel—who became a Biblical scholar of international reputation—remained extremely fat throughout his adult life: and I still cannot help associating his fatness with that *bar mitzvah* party at which he blocked my father's chances of a party by gorging himself.

From the Gymnasium at Koenigsberg my father went to Berlin University to study philosophy under Paulsen and at the same time to prosecute his rabbinical studies at the Hildesheimer Seminary, a Jewish theological college which had as its ideal the combination of strict Jewish orthodoxy and sound training in traditional rabbinics with a knowledge and appreciation of secular Western culture. The Hildesheimer ideal burned brightly in my father all his life, being eventually transformed by him into his unique Scottish-Jewish synthesis. From Berlin he went to Leipzig, where he eventually graduated A.M., Ph.D. with a thesis (in German) on the relation of David Hume's philosophy to his history. The thesis won the special prize awarded to the best German prose stylist among the graduating students of the year.

My father's native language was Yiddish, but at school in Koenigsberg he appears to have rapidly learned to look down on that language as a kind of bastard German, and he never again spoke it willingly nor did he encourage his children to learn it or to show any interest in it. For him the language of Jewish culture was Hebrew, not Yiddish, and I was brought up with an anti-Yiddish bias, not as the result of any conscious depreciation of Yiddish on my father's part but as the result of the silence and implied scorn with which he treated it. The Polish and Yiddish part of his life he put resolutely behind him, and I know virtually nothing of it. But he did talk of his student days in Germany at the beginning of the century, and I have a clear picture of him then as a studious and dedicated young man, avoiding the nonsense of German student ritual, but enjoying his glass of beer and his cigar, moving quietly and determinedly in the lively and colorful Berlin of the 1900's. He was a fine figure of a man, not tall, but well built, with abundant black hair swept back from his high forehead, a carefully shaped brown mustache waxed at the ends (he had dropped that habit before I was born) and a neat Van Dyke beard. I sometimes wonder whether during his student days he ever had any doubts about his ability to reconcile orthodox Judaism with modern secular culture, whether his philosophical studies ever momentarily shook his faith in the truth or efficacy of the rabbinical view of life. There is just the faintest suggestion of the dandy in the few early photographs of my father, which sorts oddly with his idealism and sense of dedication. Perhaps he had a struggle; perhaps there was no simple continuity between his Jewish childhood and his adult ambitions as a rabbi, but a period of doubt and hesitation lay between. This is mere speculation; what is definite is that he emerged from his student days in Germany a passionately serious and dedicated young man.

I have before me as I write a notebook of my father's dated May 15, 1908. It is marked: "Kant and Judaism. Notes," and it contains notes he made on this subject while reading in the British Museum, after he had settled in England and the year before he married. The notes are mostly in English, but occasionally he breaks into German. My father admired Kant, but was annoyed with him for his sharp criticisms of Judaism: in these notes he quotes from Kant's criticisms of Judaism and sketches out heads of a reply. Here is a characteristic extract:

Religion des guten Lebenswandel. Christianity true Religion. But Judaism is the Religion des guten Lebenswandel. Nearly all the religious commands concern life. Even to *love* God (which Kant makes such a fuss of). It never commands one to *believe,* as Christianity does. Believing (in his Godhead) saves according to the teaching of Christ. According to Jewish Law only doing right, moral (religious) actions save man. Why does not Kant see and acknowledge it. He idealises Christianity and does Judaism great injustice by misrepresenting (perhaps misunderstanding its tenets).

Or again:

"Thou shalt and thou shalt not. I am the Lord." He admits that there is a combat between the good and the evil principle. How can we expect a final victory of the good principle if not by interference of the transcendental moral power. The Divine Maker of man who takes care to enlighten man and to indicate to him the right path (of true morality) which he is bound to go. God the objective maker and adviser of man, also his judge and the framer of his destiny. He has revealed His will, His law to man, just in order that it should act as the "vehicle" which Kant takes the Christian Church to be. Christ never said anything against this.

The notebook ends with a list of German references (books and articles), followed by: "W. Wallace, 'Kant,' p. 74: 'The old man, so courageous in his books, was a coward before his King. Let age and infirmity plead for him; and let his teaching wipe away the evil of his example.'"

In his essay "Kant and Judaism," which appeared in his

book, *Aspects of Judaism,* published in 1928, my father wrote: "That Kant himself had no adequate knowledge of, or even a proper understanding for, the teachings and traditions of Judaism has been pointed out by Dr. Julius Guttmann in a monograph on 'Kant und das Judentum' (Leipzig, 1908) and by the present writer in a critical contribution to the first issue of the new *Jewish World* (April 16, 1913). But Kant's inability to understand and appreciate the tenets of Judaism has never prevented Jews from understanding and appreciating the philosophy of Kant, and to-day it is admitted by those who combine in themselves a thorough knowledge of Jewish teaching with a full appreciation of Kant's philosophical theories that there is no religious system which is so compatible with that philosopher's epistemology as well as with his ethical doctrines as the system embodied in Judaism." And so my father's lover's quarrel with Kant, like his earlier one with Hume, was eventually resolved, and the resolution is in some sense a symbol of his life.

What was my father's relation to *his* father? My grandfather migrated to England while my father was still a student, to become rabbi of an orthodox Jewish congregation —the Beth Hamedrash Hagadol—in Leeds, and from that time on my father regarded Britain as his true home. He already knew English perfectly, and after a few years in England spoke it perfectly, while my grandfather never mastered more than the merest rudiments of the language. He and my grandmother represented for me a picturesque old world in which I was not really at home. My father mediated between their world and my own, translating my grandfather's Yiddish (my grandmother could speak English) and trying to interpret the behavior of an Edinburgh schoolboy in the old man; yet I had the feeling that my father, for all his tremendous sense of family pride and loyalty and for all the great mutual affection between him and my grandfather, was not altogether happy in seeing us in this old world atmosphere. He looked forward to a Judaism no less orthodox but less involved with memories of the ghetto. We went rarely to see our grandfather. I may be wrong, but I have a suspicion that my father preferred to keep us apart.

The house in Leeds where my grandfather lived was one of a row of small nineteenth-century brick dwellings, all exactly alike, in which a number of *nouveau* middle-class hangers-on of the Industrial Revolution had once proclaimed their precarious gentility. The street had a run-down look when I knew it, and it was inhabited by very small businessmen or by miscellaneous oddities of firm respectability but moderate means. It was the kind of street one can see today in any British industrial town, shabby and tired looking, but determinedly decent. Behind the front door of any one of its houses one expected to hear thick Yorkshire accents proclaiming phrases out of J. B. Priestley or Eric Knight.

But Number 6 was different. The brass plate read, in letters almost too worn to be legible, "Rabbi J. H. Daiches"—the "J" should have been "I" since it stood for "Israel," but my grandfather considered the letters "I" and "J" interchangeable—and if you pushed open the gate and went up the narrow path that skirted the tiny apology for a front garden to the front door you were aware of approaching the entrance to a very different world from that of industrial Yorkshire. It was, one might say, an emanation which seemed be oozing out of the house, a smell, perhaps, a feeling, an atmosphere. And if you entered and went through the dark bead curtain into the small entrance hall and smelled the mingled odor of cigar smoke and Jewish cooking, you had left Yorkshire very far behind.

My grandfather as I knew him was a benevolently patriarchal figure with twinkling eyes and a white beard. Only recently, an old man who had known him in his prime told me that in his younger days in Poland he had been known as a dandy, who had oiled his beard and worn patent leather boots, and that he had given scandal to the orthodox by sending his children (my father and my uncle) to secular non-Jewish schools and universities. Between afternoon and evening services (*minchah* and *ma'arev*) at the synagogue he would go for a walk with a certain Christian civic official, with whom he would converse in Russian—a habit which caused much shaking of heads among the older people. This new light on my grandfather came as an astonishing revelation to me, who had always considered him as belonging to a ghetto world of Jewish piety and Jewish isolation. But evidently he too was a pioneer and even a rebel in his day, and tried to reconcile tradition with progress.

I saw no sign of that as a child, however. I had to watch my every movement in my grandfather's house, in case I unwittingly offended against his sense of what was proper Jewish behavior. I could never leave my head uncovered for a moment, for example. At home we always covered our heads to pray, and to say grace before and after meals, but we were never expected to keep our heads covered continually. My father wore a black skullcap when receiving members of his congregation in his study, but as the years went by he developed the habit of keeping it in his pocket throughout much of the day and diving hastily for it when the bell rang. In his father's presence he wore it continually. I remember once, seeing the two of them to-

[109]

gether in my grandfather's house, thinking how young and *modern* my father looked beside the white-bearded older rabbi. Yet at home in Edinburgh I had so often thought my father old-fashioned in manner and dress, with his black frock coat, stiff shirt front, and bow tie, and his rather formal eighteenth-century English.

In the house at Leeds the slightest daily activity seemed to partake of ritual. The great stone kitchen in the basement, where my grandmother presided amid rows of shining copper vessels, was like something out of Grimm's fairy tales, and even the dining room, with its long narrow table running the length of the room and its black horsehair sofa on one side (how the horsehair used to scratch my bare legs!) seemed more than a dining room to me. My grandfather used to shuffle in in his carpet slippers before dinner and take his place at the head of the table, where there was laid out for him a special little cloth on which were a bottle of cognac, a plate of sliced pickled herring, and a loaf of dark rye bread. He would fill himself a tot of brandy and drink it off at a gulp; then he would cut a slice of bread and eat it with the herring; and then his special cloth with everything on it was removed and the meal proper could start. I would watch this ritual with pure admiration from my place on the horsehair sofa (which was placed along one side of the table, so that we children could sit there, side by side, when having our meals: I suppose we must have been propped on something, but I don't remember that). Together with the admiration went a sense of the mystical strangeness of it all. Once, when I was almost grown up, I ventured to remark that I, too, liked pickled herring. My grandfather expressed the utmost astonishment and passed me the plate, and would not take anything himself until I had eaten rather more than I really wanted.

When I was a child I knew no Yiddish except the occasional word, referring to some aspect of daily Jewish
practice, which had found its way into our ordinary dis-
course, and an occasional phrase such as *"Ich vaiss nisht"*
(I don't know). It was only after I had learned German, in
my last years at school, that I acquired any degree of facility with the language, and even then such Yiddish as I
spoke was more German than Yiddish. (It is significant
that my father took an interest in and encouraged my
learning of German, but took no steps whatever to help
me learn Yiddish.) When I conversed with my grandfather,
which was not often, we used simple Hebrew until I was
in my teens, when he spoke in his native Yiddish and I
replied in my Germanized form of the language. Lionel
and I also used to write occasional letters to our grandfather in Hebrew. Most of them were expressions of thanks
for a birthday present (generally a pound note), and I still
remember the typical opening of such letters (I am trans-
literating roughly the Ashkenazi pronunciation): *"Hin'ni
nowsein es towdosi be'ad ha'matonoh shai-sholachto li"*
(Behold I send my thanks for the gift which you have sent
me). Later on, when I had read some of the Hebrew letters
of Achad Ha'am, I would vary this opening with elegant
locutions learned from him, such as: *"Kabeil no es towdosi
. . ."* (Receive I pray thee my thanks . . .), and I learned
too, also from Achad Ha'am, a fine opening with which to
begin a letter that should have been written some time ago.
It began "Forgive, I pray thee, my tardiness . . ." The
phrase, beginning as it did with the familiar penitential
phrase *s'lach no,* reminded me of the service of the Day of
Atonement: and it did not seem altogether improper to
address my grandfather in those terms. Yet his conversa-
tions with me violently contradicted the impression of an
aloof patriarchal character, with which I could not help

[111]

associating him in general. He had a great fondness for low jokes. I knew that he was the world's leading authority on the Jerusalem Talmud (to be distinguished from the more popular Babylonian Talmud), and that he had produced a noble edition of it with a large Hebrew commentary surrounding a tiny island of original text; so I naturally expected words of profound wisdom to fall from his venerable lips. Instead, he would inquire whether I went to the bathroom in order to drink brandy and smoke cigars secretly, or he would suggest that the sixty-five-year-old charwoman was pining for me to take her to the pictures.

I would come into his study to find him stroking his beard and poring over a huge Hebrew tome, looking the very quintessence of rabbinic grandeur. I was prepared for him to throw a question at me concerning my Hebrew knowledge and had even got up one side of a long dialogue in that language on which I was ready to embark if only he would give me the opportunity. But when I appeared he would close his book, ask me to bring him a cigar from the cupboard (like my father, he would smoke nothing but the choicest Havanas, which he got as presents from members of his congregation), and proceed to make joking or teasing remarks about kilts and bagpipes, or about girls, or clothes, or other unrabbinical subjects. Yet as soon as I left the room he was at his book again, and I could see him through the window from the back garden, with his hand on his beard and his head nodding gently, reading and meditating.

He lived in what seemed to me an almost feudal fashion. His salary must have been quite small, and in any case when I knew him he had, I believe, virtually retired, but he had retainers who would come to see him and bring cigars or a bottle of brandy or an occasional duck or

chicken. He had absolutely no money sense. My grandmother ran the financial affairs of the household, and when
she died he was at the mercy of an elderly broken-down
couple who came to live with him and look after things.
Every time I visited him he would want to present me
with a large check, and had to be restrained by my father
or some other watchful grown-up. He was quite capable of
giving me a check for much more than he had in the bank,
for I don't think he ever knew how much he had in the
bank—or indeed exactly what a bank was supposed to do.
My impression is that, at least in his later years, much of
his income was paid in kind, and he had little occasion to
handle money.

He visited us in Edinburgh only once, on the occasion of
my brother Lionel's *bar mitzvah* in March, 1924. My father
placed his study at my grandfather's disposal, and he would
sit there most of the day with one of my father's Hebrew
books. I was eleven and a half at the time, and in the midst
of a wave of enthusiasm for things Hebrew and rabbinic.
I was disconcerted to find that when my father sent me in
to recite my Hebrew verbs to my grandfather, he interrupted me before I was fairly started and the whole thing
was turned into a joke. I think now that he did not want
me to feel an obligation to be serious and show off my
Hebrew knowledge when I was with him; he wanted to
try to get to know his grandchildren and not to be simply
a criterion of piety and scholarship for them. But we never
really got to know each other; my father's optimistic faith
in the importance and the viability of British Jewish
orthodoxy, his resolute repudiation of Yiddish and its
ghetto associations, stood between my grandfather and his
grandchildren.

In my grandfather's last years he led a retired and lonely

life, never leaving his house—indeed, scarcely stirring from the big table in his study where he sat and read and dozed all day. He became too feeble to walk to the synagogue, and on Friday nights and Saturdays a dozen or so cronies would come and conduct services in his study. It was my grandmother's death that finally confirmed him in his retirement: though he lived some twelve years longer I don't think he left the house once after her funeral. When I was a student at Oxford I used to visit him on my way back to Edinburgh, and I had the feeling that the modern world, toward which he had once made such important gestures of friendship, had finally become too much for him and he had given up the attempt to keep up with it. Yet he, to me for so long the representative of the very essence of rigid old-fashioned Jewish piety, had started out as something of a rebel; by his decision on how to educate his children he had shaped the pattern both of my father's life and of my own.

The modern world caught up with both of them, my grandfather and my father. If my grandfather retreated from it in his old age, my father, with his optimistic belief in the progressive waning of anti-Semitism and the emergence of Judaism as a proud and respected part of a pluralistic European culture, was equally baffled when the rise of Hitler put the clock back in Europe. He watched with horror and incredulity the disappearance of the Germany he knew and admired—the Germany of Goethe and Kant and Beethoven—and could never understand what had really happened. True, the events of the 1930's would have confirmed him in his devotion to Britain if any such confirmation had been required, and it did intensify his feeling for Scotland, one of the few countries in Europe, he would so often declare, where the Jews had never been persecuted (though he knew that the reason for this was at least partly that the Jews reached Scotland relatively late in European history and in small numbers). But there were rumblings of fascist agitation even in Scotland; they didn't, it is true, amount to much and they represented a negligible minority of the people, but they disturbed and angered my father. He would keep an eagle eye open for letters or articles in the Scottish press which showed any trace of sympathy with the Hitlerite position, and he would reply to each with a forceful and eloquent letter to the editor. This was but an extension of his normal vigilance on behalf of the good name of the Jews in Scotland. His letters to the *Scotsman,* putting the Jewish position whenever it required to be put and always assuming the closest natural sympathy between Scottish Presbyterians and Jews, had been a feature of that newspaper since 1919. He had developed the art of Jewish apologetics to a fine point; his letters combined the shrewdness of a lawyer trained on Talmudic argument with the ringing eloquence of a preacher and the moral passion of a prophet. His letters to the *Scotsman* on such subjects as Zionism, the activities of Christian missions among Jews, the position of the Jews in Europe and in Scotland in particular, Jewish ritual slaughter, anti-Semitism, and on any topical subject with reference to which the Jewish position required defense or explanation, became perhaps my father's best-known claim to fame: they were read and admired throughout Scotland, and they did an immense amount to create a pro-Jewish public opinion in the country. The other day a railway official at Waverley Station, Edinburgh, was checking my sleeper reservation on a train out of the city and his eye was caught by the name. "Any relation of the late rabbi?" he asked. "I always used to read his letters in the *Scotsman.*"

[115]

My father enjoyed his role as a public figure and played it superbly. In his letters to the press his voice rang with the authority and the dignity of an official spokesman of his people, and similarly at public meetings in Edinburgh and throughout Scotland—at Masonic lodges, the Dunfermline Business Men's Club, the League of Nations Union, Burns clubs—he would present with eloquence and passion the Jewish view of the subject under discussion. He had not been long in Edinburgh before he became known as one of the city's most distinguished public speakers, who could be counted on to make forceful oratorical contributions to any humanitarian or liberal cause. Of course he spoke too at Zionist meetings and at Jewish fund-raising occasions of all kinds, and looking back I seem to see an endless round of such occasions, but I think it was the speeches he made as a representative Jewish spokesman before non-Jewish and mixed audiences that gave him most satisfaction. For that, in his view, was an important part of the function of the modern Orthodox Jewish rabbi—to speak up for his people with dignity and equality before his fellow citizens.

This side of my father's activities can perhaps best be summed up by quoting four letters to him that I have found among a mass of his miscellaneous papers. Here is the first:

LODGE QUEEN'S EDINBURGH RIFLES
(THE ROYAL SCOTS)
No. 1253

"Mansfield"

Rev. Dr. Salis Daiches   74 Fergus Drive
17 Crawfurd Road,   Glasgow, N.W.
EDINBURGH, 9.   20th December, 1935
Reverend Sir and Brother,

I was very pleased to learn from our Secretary that you had

[116]

accepted our invitation to give the oration at our Burns' Festival. I must thank you very much for the honour you are doing us and I am looking forward to meeting you again on that evening.

With cordial greetings,

Yours sincerely and fraternally,

Alex Mennie

The second is from the editor of the Edinburgh *Evening News*. My father had evidently written to him offering congratulations on some anniversary either of the paper or of the editor personally:

EDINBURGH EVENING NEWS

18 Market Street
Edinburgh 1

12 February, 1936

Rev. Dr. Salis Daiches, A.M., Ph.D.,
17 Crawfurd Road,
Edinburgh. 9.

Dear Rabbi,

You have sent me a wonderful letter of congratulation, full of encouragement and good will. I appreciate especially what you say about the Jewish community in Scotland and in my own town of Edinburgh. I know I have many friends among the Jews, and if at any time there is anything I can do to help their cause, you have only to come up here.

I am sure Mrs. McPhail will be very pleased with the very kind letter you have sent us.

With every kind wish,

I remain

yours sincerely

Walter McPhail

Editor

The third is more routine, and typical of hundreds:

THE LEAGUE OF NATIONS UNION
(Greenock Branch)

Hon Secretary:
Mr. J. W. Ashford,
18 Kilblain Street,
Greenock.
Phone No. 118.

Rev. dear Sir,

Thank you for your letter. My Committee has not yet fixed a date for the Annual Meeting, but would be pleased to arrange a date suitable to you. . . .

The first time I am in Edinburgh, I shall make a point of seeing you.

With thanks,
I am,
Yours truly,

J. W. Ashford
Hon. Secretary

Rev. Dr. Daiches,
17 Crawfurd Road,
EDINBURGH, 9.

Across the foot of this letter my father has written the date, "17th March," and on that day he addressed the Greenock Branch of the League of Nations Union.

The fourth letter is in many ways the most interesting:

NIDDRIE MAINS WORKERS' INSTITUTE

17 Harewood Drive
Craigmillar
EDINBURGH.

2nd December, 1935.

Dear Sir,

I have been instructed to write and ask you, if you would kindly permit an interview to the above organisation. We are a

[118]

body of Workers in the area, who have up to the present time been raising to build a hall.

Sir we intend to commence the building in about a months time, the interview is for the porpose [*sic*] of asking you to honour our attempt at the opening cermoney [*sic*] and cutting of first turf for us. Hoping to be able to explain our aims and object to you in our interview.

I am yours sincerely

J. P. Ferguson
Secy.

My father did in due course cut the first turf for the new workers' hall, and I think few things gave him more satisfaction.

If this side of my father's activities took him considerably beyond the path of duty trod by my grandfather in the performance of the more traditional activities of a Jewish rabbi, it must not be thought for a moment that my father in any way neglected those traditional activities. He would receive almost daily visits from the older members of his congregation in search of guidance on some intricate matter of Jewish law: whether a chicken could be considered kosher if a pin had been found stuck in some delicate part of its internal organs, or what was the correct procedure on the part of a bachelor who wanted to get out of marrying his deceased brother's widow. These matters he dealt with scrupulously and conscientiously, becoming on such occasions the old-fashioned administrator of rabbinical law in all its logical nicety. His very appearance seemed to change when he gave an audience of this kind: he allowed his shoulders to hunch forward a little and spoke, reluctantly and in his Germanized fashion, the Yiddish which was the speech of his visitor; and of course his skullcap was always on his head. This side of him was always uppermost when he spoke to the older, foreign-born members of his congregation: with the native-born generation he was brisker and altogether more modern; the singsong tones of Talmudic exposition gave way to a more resounding rhetorical note or to the reasonable "let's-argue-this-out-together" tone of twentieth-century inquiry.

Before my father came to Edinburgh there were two Jewish congregations in the city, one consisting entirely of older, foreign-born members whose native language was Yiddish, and the other, though also orthodox, having a considerable proportion of Scottish-born members who did not believe that to practice Judaism meant to duplicate exactly the kind of life their fathers had led in the East European ghetto. My father made it a condition of accepting his "call" that it should come jointly from both congregations, and when he arrived in Edinburgh his first task was to weld the two into a unity. For some years they continued to worship in different synagogues, that of the foreign-born group being an old and drafty hall in what was pretty much a slum area of the city. The other synagogue, the converted chapel in Graham Street, clearly represented the wave of the future, and its congregation grew while the other's declined. My father would worship and preach on Saturdays at the Graham Street Shul, though he would visit the other (known as the Central Shul) at regular intervals and preach there in Yiddish. After a few years the Central Shul closed down and Graham Street accommodated both congregations. My father's real ambition was to build a splendid new synagogue in a pleasant part of the city, a synagogue which could easily accommodate all the Jews in Edinburgh and would, in addition, have an attached *Beth Hamedrash* where the older and more traditional members could pray three times daily and conduct their Talmudic study circle. This ambition was finally realized after immense effort, and the new synagogue in Salisbury Road was opened with full civic honors in 1932. Its opening was a high point in my father's career, for here was represented the union of the old and the new in a common Jewish orthodoxy; the building took its place worthily amid the architecture of Edinburgh and signified that Edinburgh Jews played their part with integrity and dignity and with the respect of their neighbors in the life of their city.

The shadows cast by Hitler's Germany were soon to obscure the Jewish horizon completely; after 1934 there was little cause for optimism even among men as naturally optimistic as my father. 1934, too, was the year when he and my mother celebrated their silver wedding anniversary, the year when we moved into a new house, the first my father had ever owned, and the year when I graduated with first-class honors at Edinburgh University, to my father's immense satisfaction. So altogether the years 1932 to 1934 represent the watershed, as it were, of my father's career. After that, the world he had counted on began to disappear beneath his feet; anti-Semitism, which I had been brought up to believe was a phenomenon of the bad old days that would never recur, would rise to unprecedented heights in Germany, and I myself began for the first time to doubt profoundly the whole basis of the creed in which I had been brought up. (Perhaps I should interpolate here that that basis, from a belief in which my father apparently never deviated one jot throughout his life, was that the Law was given to Moses by divine revelation on Mount Sinai, that this revelation was unique, and central in human history, and that the function of the Jewish people had been to receive and transmit and would be to foster and develop the revealed Law.)

It had been a hard climb to the summit represented by the opening of the new synagogue. The position which my father had won for himself, and through himself for his people, in Scotland was achieved by the continual expenditure of energy, writing, speaking, debating, counseling, planning, being diplomatic here and righteously indignant there, moving continuously between platform, pulpit, study, and meeting room. Our house was in some respects like a public institution; callers were liable to arrive at any time. My father had to keep up a style of living which his modest salary made extremely difficult. The Edinburgh Hebrew Congregation was small—about two thousand souls—and not wealthy, and could not afford to pay its spiritual leader much of a stipend. My father, in virtue of his personality and abilities, had made himself the unofficial spiritual leader of all Jews in Scotland; but in sober fact he was but the rabbi of a small congregation. The result of this was that while the outside world regarded him as the Jewish equivalent of the Archbishop of Canterbury or at least of the Moderator of the Church of Scotland, and expected him to live accordingly, my father had to manage somehow on his small income. We had to live in a large and thoroughly genteel house in a residential part of the city, we had to dress well, we had to subscribe decently to public charities. My father was thus always harassed by financial worries, always haunted by unpaid bills. And though somehow the bills always got paid eventually and no visible sign of financial stringency was ever open to the public eye, the continuous strain must have worn down both my parents.

There was another kind of strain, more wearing than

financial worry. My father, in the course of his successful attempts to make himself a real leader of his people and to build up a public conception of the Jew in Scotland as the respected member of an important element in a pluralistic culture, aroused some bitter jealousies and made some implacable enemies. A number of petty busybodies who had made a profession of exploiting disputes among different sections of the community were taken aback at my father's policy of uniting all the Jews of Edinburgh into one congregation (it was, indeed, a unique policy, and the Edinburgh Hebrew Congregation remains a unique Jewish congregation in Britain) and deliberately set out to make trouble for him. On one occasion a couple of them attacked my father's silk hat as it hung in a cloakroom while he was at a meeting, and ripped it to pieces. This was one of the more dramatic episodes, but it was, in fact, less serious than the continual attempts to undermine my father's position, to discredit him in the eyes of Jew and Christian alike, that this small group kept making for some years. My father, who had conducted his side of the business with a fine dignity, won in the end, as he was bound to, though for some years a small group of malcontents worshiped separately in a hired room (known among the other Edinburgh Jews as the "Bolshie Shul") in a mood of spiteful piety.

All this, of course, was worrying, but most worrying of all was the affair that became known as the "Levinson case." One day in the 1920's a gentleman calling himself Rabbi Levinson turned up at Edinburgh and made contact with the members of the "Bolshie Shul." He began to make large claims about his rabbinical distinction and jurisdiction, and eventually my father, after making some investigations into the man's character and history, denounced him as a trouble-making imposter and wrote a letter to the London *Jewish Chronicle* pointing out that "Rabbi" Levinson was no rabbi and warning British Jews against him. (At least, I think that is what happened, but it may be that the *Chronicle* came to the same conclusion independently: it certainly published a warning against Levinson.) Levinson then proceeded to bring an action for libel against both my father and the *Jewish Chronicle*. This was an immense shock to my father, who knew perfectly well that Levinson was a rogue and an imposter but knew also that this would not be easy to prove in a court of law. And of course my father had no money to fight a legal action. But the action had to be fought, and my father engaged the best legal representatives available, trusting that he would win and be awarded costs.

As the case proceeded Levinson's counsel submitted as evidence of his being a genuine rabbi a large number of documents, some of them signed by rabbinical authorities of international reputation. All these were testimonials to the scholarship, piety, and rabbinic distinction of Levinson. When my father's counsel saw these documents, he thought the case was over: what answer could there be to such evidence? My father, however, persuaded his counsel to ask leave to borrow the documents for a week (they had been deposited in court), and leave was granted. He read them over very carefully, and as he read he noticed a number of things. One of the most impressive documents was signed by Rabbi Kook, the late Chief Rabbi of Palestine. Now my father knew Rabbi Kook, and corresponded with him; in fact, he had a letter from him on his desk at that time. He compared the signature of his own letter with that on the document brought by Levinson, and found that the two were quite different. A closer investigation made it clear that both the signature and the seal were forged. With this clue in his possession, my father went carefully through the other documents. Many of them were clearly genuine; but these did not prove anything except that the writer thought Levinson was a nice man. But every one of the documents purporting to come from a rabbinical authority was suspect. One purported to come from a town in Poland which my father was sure did not exist. Another came from the head of a continental Yeshivah that he had never heard of. One was supposed to be from a rabbi in some small town in the interior of Australia.

My father informed his counsel that in his view all the Levinson documents which seemed to prove that he was in fact a genuine rabbi were either forged or had been tampered with; the numerous others which were genuine doing no harm to my father's case at all. The eminent legal authority at first refused to believe this. No man, he protested, could be guilty of such criminal folly. But my father insisted, and urged that before the documents were returned to court they should be photostated for further study. This was done, under protest from the legal advisers. Soon afterward, Levinson asked for leave to take the documents temporarily out of court, since he was applying for a position with a Jewish congregation in Wales and needed the testimonials. He was given leave to withdraw them for a short period. When they were put back, as they were a week or so later, my father asked his counsel to borrow them again, briefly. What, asked the advocate, could he possibly want with them again? My father pressed the point, and the documents were soon in his hands again. He noticed at once that the bundle felt lighter. He examined them carefully: every one of the forged and suspect documents was gone! When my father rang up his lawyer to tell him this, the good man was at first incredulous, but seeing was believing, and he was soon brought to realize what had happened. What had happened, of course, was that Levinson, when he heard that my father had been examining the documents, realized that he might have discovered the forgeries and thought it prudent, even at the risk of destroying his case, to withdraw them. What he did not know was that my father and his defending counsel had photographs of all the documents he had originally submitted.

Well might my father have said, in Biblical and Cromwellian phrase, "The Lord has delivered him into my hand." For that was the beginning of the end of Levinson, whose case crumpled when faced with the fact of the missing documents. When my father's counsel drew the attention of the judge in court to the absence from the returned bundle of the very documents which he was prepared to prove were forgeries, the judge sharply asked Levinson for an explanation. Levinson said that the missing testimonials and diplomas had been accidentally destroyed by his landlady when she was clearing up his room. The coincidence of the landlady's having accidentally destroyed just those documents which my father was prepared to prove were forgeries was too much for anybody to credit, and it was not long before Levinson was completely exposed and the case was concluded. Judgment, with costs, was awarded to my father, and the judge said some severe words about the behavior of Levinson's solicitor.

This was, of course, a very satisfactory conclusion for my father. Before the discovery that the forged documents were missing, the court was preparing to send out a commission of inquiry to interrogate the persons alleged to have given these testimonials to Levinson—and this could have cost my father a fortune, though presumably it would have been charged to Levinson if my father had won and been awarded costs. But though my father did win and was awarded costs, Levinson skipped the country (it was thought that he went to America) and avoided paying a penny, so that eventually my father's solicitors had to come back to him to settle the bill. Fortunately, the *Jewish Chronicle*, who had been joint defendant with my father and who had been cleared as a result of my father's astuteness in handling the matter, recognized what they owed to him and offered to settle his legal expenses—an offer which was gratefully accepted.

Throughout the long months during which the Levinson case dragged on, my father continued to fulfill all his normal duties, preaching, lecturing, writing, advising. We children had no idea at the time of the great weight of anxiety that must have been pressing upon him. We knew all about the case, but we thought of it as something thrilling and amusing. It never occurred to us that if by any chance my father had lost, his whole reputation and career would have been ruined, his whole life's ambitions destroyed. I remember seeing the photographed documents lying on his desk in his study and reading through some of them with casual interest: I recollect some brief notes to the effect that Levinson had successfully performed circumcisions. And I remember one evening my father sitting in his chair by the fire after dinner, stroking his mustache in the way he had and looking unusually worried. But for the most part he gave no sign of the strain upon him. Even at the end, with the enormous relief of the judgment, he remained calm and went on with his arduous daily duties. His victory was another proof of the rightness of his way of life, proof that God would not see the righteous forsaken. As for me, I never doubted that my father would win—I took it as a matter of course—and when I heard of the judgment there came into my head the sentence I had read in history books, spoken by loyal subjects after the execution of a traitor: "So perish all the King's enemies!"

Long after the Levinson case was over it continued to provide my father with an enthralling after-dinner story, with which he would regale guests. He would tell it well, building up carefully to the climax of the discovery of the forged documents and letting the tension die away somewhat before he came to the second climax, the discovery of the absence of the suspected documents from the returned bundle. My father took a naïve pride in his own part in it all, and stressed the fact that his counsel was reluctant to borrow the documents in the first place and still more so to borrow them a second time. I last heard him tell the story in December, 1944, when I was home briefly on leave from a war job. It was a Friday night, and there were guests at dinner, including the Senior Jewish Chaplain to the Forces, Rabbi Brodie (now Chief Rabbi of the British Empire). I had heard my father tell the story many times before, but it never became tedious to me. This time I heard it with peculiar pleasure: I was on my first visit back to Edinburgh in five years, having been cut off on the other side of the Atlantic by the war and being able to get back now only because I was flown across the Atlantic on British Government service by the R.A.F. Transport Command. It was like old days again—Friday night, guests for dinner, my father telling of the Levinson case. I noticed, however, that he got one or two of the details wrong, and though he corrected himself, he had not the firm grip on the story that he used to have. I looked across the table at him: his right arm was in plaster, the result of a nasty fracture he had received some weeks before when he had been knocked down by a lorry while about to board a tramcar; his face showed heavy lines of fatigue, and his voice too sounded tired. I did not know then that he was a dying man, and would live only a few more months. But I did reflect how satisfactory it was that the greatest threat to his career had long passed into the realm of anecdote, and I thought that Hitler, too, was now in sight of his end and looked forward to the time when this black shadow would pass completely from the Jewish sky and my father could relax at last in a world that showed, in spite of everything, the eventual triumph of right over might. That phrase, "the triumph of right over might," was a favorite one of my father's, and he used it often during war. He died on May 2, 1945, one day after Hitler and three weeks after Roosevelt.

CHAPTER 6

---◀◉▶---

There were only three years between my elder brother Lionel and my younger sister Sylvia: I came in the middle, exactly as much younger than Lionel as I was older than Sylvia. My middle position had certain advantages. Lionel was the one who had to pioneer the new situations, and I followed where he had been. He was a year ahead of me at school, and encountered new subjects and new masters a year before I did, so that by the time I had to face them they were familiar to me from innumerable descriptions and anecdotes. Sometimes I even had Lionel's notes in front of me when a teacher was giving a new lesson; I remember on one occasion having on the desk before me a set of the superb history summaries that Dr. Brydon, one of the finest teachers of history to schoolboys who ever lived, used to put on the blackboard. I had got the summaries from Lionel, who had been in Dr. Brydon's class the year before, and was able to answer every question in exactly the form which the master wanted. He soon discovered that I had an old set of his notes, and cheerfully allowed me to display my knowledge by starting a sentence and then turning to me to finish it. (*E.g.*, Brydon: "The first defect in the Congress of Vienna was—" He turned to me. Me: "It ignored the rising claims of national feeling.") This sort of thing was of course useful, though it grew progressively less so as I went up the school and grew more independent in my attitude to the various subjects. Other advantages of being the middle child were that I was in some degree insulated from the emotional pressure that parents in spite of themselves direct against the oldest and the youngest among their children, and that I was on the whole left more to myself. I was the youngest (or rather, the younger) for not quite eighteen months, and then Sylvia was born, the first girl, and a remarkably pretty one at that, with the result that any claims I had to special attention disappeared at once. Not that I was ever conscious of being less attended to than Lionel or Sylvia; but I think, on looking back, that in some subtle ways I probably was.

There is, in Jewish tradition as in many other traditions, a peculiar *mystique* attached to the oldest son. Lionel was the first-born male, and as such he had certain privileges that I was denied. I can hear now my father's voice saying: "Lionel should do it: he is the eldest." Duties as well as privileges were involved, and I don't think Lionel cared particularly for either. I grew used to the notion that Lionel was in the nature of things more privileged than I, and, unless my memory deceives me, I very rarely resented this. Perhaps I did, though, unconsciously; else why should I have so often prided myself secretly on my greater sensitivity to my father's moods and ideals? There was a significant difference in temperament between Lionel and myself. At school he was indolent and unambitious, while I worked hard and was always anxious to excel. He got out of as many religious duties as he could, although, of course, during the period of our childhood he no more than the rest of us would have thought of actively defying orthodox standards by riding on a tramcar on a Saturday or eating improper food. Praying, for example: we were expected to daven (pray) regularly and at length each morning, and, after we had reached the age of thirteen, lay tephillin (put on phylacteries) and go through the whole vast series of morning prayers before breakfast. Lionel, who always got up at the last possible moment, gabbled through the Sh'ma (the most important of these prayers, but very short) in record time, and let it go at that. I felt an absolute obligation to start at the very beginning and go right through to the end without missing a word. It was a psychological compulsion, of the kind that made Dr. Johnson touch every second lamppost as he walked through the streets of London, and had little to do with piety. If by negligence or haste I found I had omitted even a word, I felt I had to go back to the beginning and start the whole thing over again. I reached the stage where I could rush through some sixty pages of Hebrew in ten minutes flat, without distorting a single word (the pages, I admit, were the small duodecimo pages of Singer's prayer book).

I also felt a certain compulsion to be at the Saturday morning service at the very beginning, though few people came or were expected to come at the start, and the larger part of the congregation arrived for the "Reading of the Law," which was a good halfway through the proceedings. It was, like all Jewish services except the pleasant Friday night one (always my favorite for its plaintive melodies as well as its sensible length), long, beginning about 9:30 and going on until about 12:00. My father, of course, had to be there at the beginning, and I always liked to go with him. Lionel, who got up later, used to arrive about 10 o'clock. My father never liked this separate arrival of Lionel and me, and was not particularly eager for me to come so early. Once, I remember, as I was preparing to start out with him, he suggested that I stay and wait for Lionel, so that we would both arrive together. I think I was eleven or so at the time. The suggestion upset me, for some reason I felt unable to explain, and when my father repeated that he expected me to wait and come later with Lionel, I found myself, inexplicably, bursting into tears. I am not quite sure what my emotions really were—nothing so simple as frustrated piety. I had set my heart on going with my father and being in shul for the beginning of the service. He was astonished to find me in tears. "What, *crying?*" he said. "Foolish boy. Come along, then." And I dried my tears and went along with him. After that there was never any question about it: I always went with him at the beginning.

Piety did play some part in my childhood praying, however. I made up a long prayer for myself, partly in Hebrew and partly in English, to be recited under the bedclothes after I had got into bed at night. It was a curious mixture of echoes from the regular Hebrew night prayer with snatches from a variety of other sources. It began with a request to be spared bad dreams (I was cursed with horrid nightmares as a child, and often brought my parents upstairs in a hurry with my fearful screams), went on to recite the *Sh'ma,* continued with bits of psalms and hymns, and ended with an original composition in English requesting a blessing on the whole family. It was quite a long performance altogether, and the more tired I was the more compulsion I felt to go through the whole thing. Sometimes, when I was exceptionally tired, I allowed myself an abbreviated form, but in most cases I then found my con-

[133]

science (or something within me) unsatisfied and had to proceed to the complete set of prayers after all. Between the ages of about eleven and fifteen I became a conscientious prayer in shul, making it a point of honor not to skip anything. The real endurance test came on the Day of Atonement, when there was an enormous collection of prayers to be got through which hardly anybody thought of reciting entirely: I would go through them all. It was only in my late teens when I had examined some of the prayers and found them superstitious or in some way offensive to my increasingly critical mind, that I gave up the habit of tackling the complete prayer book.

Lionel's attitude to these matters seemed to me at the time much more careless. He did what he had to in the way of praying and religious duties, and omitted whatever he could get away with omitting. Not that he was at that age in any way a skeptic; he accepted his religion easily and naturally, but, being a schoolboy, he took the normal schoolboy's line of doing the minimum in anything that involved work or application. His attitude to religion, it seems to me, has not much changed since then. He has not, so far as I am aware, gone through any crisis of belief or conscience of the kind I went through before I first allowed myself to omit even the most trivial of orthodox Jewish observances; he simply omits what he can't be bothered to do, and preserves a genial allegiance to the family tradition without being bound by it when it doesn't suit him. There is something admirably civilized about this, though I was sometimes startled by it when I was younger.

Lionel, Sylvia, and I naturally played together a great deal, and Lionel and I alone to an even greater extent. His attitude to me was a mixture of loyalty and a most exas-

[134]

perating teasing. He teased me sometimes to distraction. I remember one occasion, when I was twelve or thirteen, he amused himself by drawing up a contract in which I was made to hand over to him something of mine that he wanted. Naturally, I refused to sign it, so he secretly cut my signature out of the cover of my French notebook and gummed it onto the contract. This was, of course, a joke; he never intended to hold me to the contract; but when I found my French notebook mutilated—it was a new one, and I had prided myself on keeping it with scrupulous neatness—I was seized with a raging sense of injustice that vented itself in howling abuse. To my further infuriation, my parents reproved me for yelling and screaming, and seemed uninterested in the monstrous injustice I had suffered; to them, I was simply being very naughty and that was that. I remember the evening clearly: my father had been away, lecturing I think, somewhere in England, and had just returned, presenting both Lionel and me with a penknife. It was with his new penknife that Lionel cut out my name from the notebook. The atmosphere of happy family reunion was abruptly shattered by my raging on discovering the state of my notebook, and I recall thinking bitterly as, denied all redress, I went fuming upstairs to my room, that the incident had spoiled what would have been a happy evening.

On another occasion I remember that Lionel and a boy who lived in the next street (his name sticks in my mind as Bill Revans, but I may have got it wrong) jointly persuaded me to shake some pennies out of my little green money box and to spend the money on a large ice cream. Such behavior was unthinkable in our family: we children saved our weekly pennies (later, threepenny pieces) and the idea of spending them on sweets or ice cream was shocking. I allowed myself to be persuaded, bought the ice cream, and gave Lionel and Bill Revans the bulk of it. Later that day Lionel calmly informed my father of what I had done. I think it was sheer pyschological curiosity on his part; he wanted to know how my father would react; but of course I was furious at this treachery. However, my father's reaction was surprisingly mild; he simply said that I shouldn't have done it and turned to his work, and that was the end of that.

But with all his teasing Lionel was fundamentally loyal. His sense of family unity was very deep—to this day I think he depends on it emotionally to a greater extent than any of us—and in a crisis he could aways be depended on. I recall two incidents, widely separated in time, which illustrate his combination of day-to-day teasing with fundamental loyalty. The first occurred when I was about fourteen or fifteen, and was writing a great deal of verse, which I kept in a fat dark-blue notebook. Once, after I had entered a new composition in the book and was about to put it away in the drawer where I kept it, Lionel noticed what I was doing and made some offensive remark about my "poems." I was angered, but instead of saying anything I calmly took up the notebook again and wrote down on the last page exactly what he had said. I headed the page: "Nasty remarks that people have made about my poems." Lionel's curiosity was aroused, and he demanded to know what I was doing. I told him, and explained that he would look a frightful fool when I was a famous poet and the disparaging remarks that he had made about my work were revealed. To my surprise, he took my words more seriously than I myself did, and reproved me for showing a mean spirit and bearing malice: it was unfair, he protested, that casual words spoken in haste should be recorded for posterity. I was touched, and tore out the page.

The other incident occurred either in my last year at school or in my first year at Edinburgh University. I had written a number of sketches, both words and music, songs from which Lionel and I often sang to entertain guests. Lionel had the idea that one of them should actually be presented publicly on a proper stage. I protested that this was not feasible, but Lionel persisted. He went round to all the boys of our own age that we knew—which meant, in fact, a handful of sons of members of the Edinburgh Jewish community—and aroused their interest by himself singing through the whole of one of the sketches, taking all the parts in turn. I was too shy to go into any of the boys' houses, but remained outside in the street while Lionel went through his performance. He convinced enough people of the merit of the piece to have it put on by a Jewish young people's club of which we were members (the Edinburgh Junior Jewish Club it was called, and later the name was changed to the Edinburgh Young Jewish Society). Lionel collected the cast, arranged for the hire of the hall, and produced the show, with an energy and fervor unusual for him. It was a great success, and was followed the next year by another. Never once did he show the slightest jealousy of my status as author and composer: for him, the whole thing showed what the family could do.

Lionel, as I have said, was never as good at his studies as I was, either at school or at home with his Hebrew. He gave up the piano quite early because, although he was musical and had a good voice, he could not be bothered with it and had not enough natural facility with the instrument to enable him to cover up his lack of practicing.

But he was much better with his hands than I was, and did extra woodwork at school, a subject for which he won several prizes. He also won, year after year, the school's annual elocution prize. He had—and has—a fine voice and a clear, resonant utterance. It was not until he went to the university that he realized his natural gifts as a public speaker. Temperamentally different from my father as he was in so many ways, he inherited his rhetorical flair. In fact, we both did, though in quite different ways. Neither of us ever found any difficulty in speaking impromptu with considerable force and eloquence; if Lionel can today walk into court after half-an-hour's rapid looking over of a vast mass of papers and deliver, without a single note, a powerful and at the same time meticulously logical defense of his client, and if I can walk into a lecture room and talk for an hour, similarly without a note, about Renaissance criticism or the problems faced by the modern novelist, we both owe our talent to our father's inheritance. Lionel is the more rhetorical, preferring to set things out in sharply contrasting black and white, and not afraid to draw on sheer sentimentality when it will help his cause; my tone is more conversational, and I think, because of my different kind of training, that I am the more intellectually self-conscious.

In spite of the fact that Lionel was not as good at his studies as I was, my father always seemed to pay more attention to his progress at school and at the university. When Lionel started Greek, my father went out and bought a copy of Pope's Homer (a second-hand copy from Grant's), presenting it to him with the remark that he was never to use it as a "crib," but only to read in a general way after he had done his translation from the Greek for himself. (It did not take Lionel long to discover that it was impossible to use Pope's Homer as a crib!) Lionel's career was discussed more fully and more often than mine was. When, on one occasion, Lionel came near enough to the top of his class at school to win a prize, my father was so pleased that he bought him a set of chessmen, and wrote an inscription to him in ink on the wooden box. This outraged my sense of justice. I pointed out to my father that I had consistently done better at school than Lionel had, and that I had never received any recognition of that sort; was it fair to present Lionel with a box of chessmen for getting a prize in a "B" class when I was regularly doing even better in an "A" class? My father recognized the justice of my protest; he took out his penknife and scratched out the "Lionel" on the inscription, putting in its stead (with some squeezing) "Lionel and David." But the wood was rough where he had scratched it, and the ink ran. The box still exists, with "Lionel and David" merged into an indeterminate blob of ink.

As I grew older, and my literary and academic interests increased, I found more to talk about with my father than Lionel did, and the balance was redressed. It must not be thought that in any case there was any question of my father deliberately paying more attention to Lionel. It was for the most part just that he was the first-born, and he arrived at each of the milestones of childhood progress before I did; so naturally a greater fuss was made when he got there. There were more and fancier cakes at his *bar mitzvah* party than at mine, and my grandfather and one of my father's sisters came up to Edinburgh for the occasion, while nobody came up for mine. And my father's congregation produced handsomer presents for Lionel than they did for me. After all, when an occasion of that sort happens a second time, the first fine careless rapture has been lost. When, coming home from shul after singing the relevant portion of the law and prophets on my *bar mitzvah* (it is traditional for a boy on attaining his *bar mitzvah* to give such a performance in the synagogue), somebody congratulated me on the fine way I had done my part, my mother, I think quite unconsciously, said: "Ah, but you should have heard Lionel." Lionel probably did sing better at his *bar mitzvah* than I did at mine; he had an excellent voice, and it was still a clear childish treble, while my voice, not naturally so resonant as his, was already on the point of breaking when I was thirteen; but my mother's remark, which I have never forgotten, stays in my mind as a symbol of the birthright of the first-born in a Jewish family.

All this helped to encourage my proud sense of being lonely and different, which grew upon me during my adolescence. But it did nothing to lessen that deeply affectionate and almost protective feeling toward my parents that I have already described. The image of my father as a lonely idealist in a naughty world and of my mother as a frail beauty in a dangerous world grew steadily stronger throughout my adolescent years. And for years I had a strong feeling that I, alone of us children, was destined to take the torch from my father's hand and help to transmit it down the generations. I sometimes thought of myself as Jacob and Lionel as Esau, or even of myself as Joseph, and once lay awake all night wondering whether I might not be the Messiah. Yet it is quite probable that the night after my messianic meditation, rich with all the emotions of Jewish history, I was imagining myself in full Highland dress participating (to the sound of the bagpipes) in some splendid assertion of Scotland's nationhood.

How difficult it is to tell the truth and not be misleading! It might be imagined from what I have written above that I had a grievance against Lionel for being the elder son and against my parents for treating him as such. But I had no shadow of such a grievance (in spite of individual instances such as that of the chessmen) nor did I ever really believe that Lionel got preferential treatment from my parents. It was, after all, the simple fact that he *was* the eldest, and that was that. I accepted the fact with the simple pragmatism of childhood. Though I was easily stirred to a sense of injustice about little things—as most children are—the idea of a general grievance against the state of affairs would have been inconceivable to me. As a family, we were as united as a family could be, loyal, proud of each other and of our traditions, maintaining a united front against the world.

Sylvia, who often joined in our play and was very much of a tomboy as a little girl, must have had her own secret life, of which I knew nothing. She was bright at school, talkative and clear-headed at home. There was a streak of sternness in her character which developed as she grew older; she had a strong will, the kind of clear, logical mind one thinks of as masculine, and at the same time more than her share of feminine attractiveness. From an early age she learned to help Mother in the kitchen, and often when Mother was unwell she would pretty well look after the house, managing her schoolwork at the same time. Brothers, of course, never think of whether a sister is pretty or not, and I remember the shock of surprise when I saw her in her first grown-up party dress and realized how very attractive she was.

My father had old-fashioned notions about her. As he watched her develop from a lively *gamine* into a beautiful woman he thought of her marrying—at the age of about twenty-one, say—and expected that if suitable Jewish young men were brought to her attention she would fall in love with one of them. But Sylvia had an immense scorn for that whole approach to marriage. Indeed, she had an immense scorn for a lot of things. Her downright, logical mind, her ruthless intellectual honesty, her refusal to compromise an inch on any subject whatsoever, made her a most formidable debating opponent. She could see no use in the conventional hypocrisies of social life. "Why should I talk to a man as though I liked him if I think he's a fool?" she would burst out. "Why *should* I?" was one of her favorite questions. "Why should I *pretend?* It's dishonest. You don't want me to be dishonest, do you?" The result was that her social manner was for long gauche and unhappy, and she frightened to death innumerable young men. Her reaction to any of the conventional gallantries was absolutely devastating. Several young men were imported from Jewish communities in other cities for her to look over and if possible fall in love with, though of course she was not supposed to know that it had all been arranged. Some of them were eligible in the highest degree, intelligent, personable, and wealthy. But Sylvia froze them all off. They fell in love with *her* all right, which was not difficult, for she was a real beauty; but they had to retreat discomfited before her stony indifference. They brought flowers, invited her out to dinner-dances, called on her; she turned scornfully away, to devote herself to her modern language studies. The whole idea of having men brought along for her approval outraged her, and she knew perfectly well what was going on. My poor father was bewildered and upset. "Don't you *want* to get married?" he once asked her plaintively after she had sent away one of the most eligible young men of all. The answer to that question was that she was not thinking about or ready for marriage then, and in any case she certainly would not want to get married at all in that way. Nothing was further from my father's thoughts than to force her affections; he simply did not see why she did not fall in love with at least one of the suitors provided. He knew that the Jewish community in Edinburgh was small and the number of suitable local men strictly limited, and that was why he took pains to have suitors from other cities brought to her attention. Often eligible suitors turned up of their own accord. One attractive but shy young man from another city saw her when they were both attending an Edinburgh Jewish wedding and was violently smitten, but he made the horrid mistake of sending his father to my father to negotiate on his behalf. To be treated for in that way was for Sylvia the ultimate outrage, and that young man was sunk from the beginning. He did not give up easily. His father kept coming to my father with ever more urgent messages and promises of ever richer endowments (the family was very wealthy): Sylvia would have a car and chauffeur of her own, a fantastic weekly amount to spend, a house built to her own specifications. Like a poor girl tempted by a wicked king in a fairy tale, Sylvia turned everything down; eventually, in despair, the young man went and found (or perhaps had his father find for him) another bride.

Sylvia took modern languages at Edinburgh University, and emerged as an excellent romance philologist. Her four-year course necessitated her spending a year in France, and she taught in a school in Douai for her third year, eating only vegetarian food and scrupulously maintaining her Jewish orthodoxy in a French Catholic establishment. As is almost inevitable in such cases, she found

[143]

herself, in the course of her years at Edinburgh University, becoming attached to a non-Jewish young man, one of her fellow students, who was much in love with her. But she knew where her duty lay. She would not marry a specially imported Jewish suitor; but equally she would not consider for a moment marrying out of the faith, with all the terrible consequences for her parents. That young man was also sent firmly away, though I suspect it was not as easy a business as dismissing the tame millionaires. A year or two later, she met one of my fellow students at Oxford, an extremely able young man of sound Jewish background but with no money at all; and eventually she married him, to become the wife of a university teacher of philosophy. She wanted a small, private wedding in Oxford, and it was only my mother's strong persuasion that led her to submit to a public wedding in Edinburgh. As for my father, his new son-in-law was a philosopher and was well versed in orthodox Jewish tradition; he was content; but, to everybody's astonishment, he quaintly objected that the young man had not asked him for Sylvia's hand in marriage before approaching Sylvia herself.

My father had an ambivalent attitude toward Sylvia's academic career. He was immensely proud of her success, and boasted about it to his friends, but he saw it all as a preliminary to settling down and making somebody a good wife. It was the same with his attitude to my mother: he was proud of her musical abilities and intellectual interests, and boasted about them when he could, but he did not expect her to take them very seriously. A woman's first and essential duty was to be a good wife and mother. Sylvia taught for a while at a school in Oxford before she married, and after her marriage—early in the war—was assistant lecturer in French at University College, London, before taking a war job with the Treasury. My father was proud of her activities in these spheres, but I think he was somewhat uneasy, too, and was waiting for the time when she would leave all that and produce children. He died before either of Sylvia's two children was born, so he was denied this comfort.

Meanwhile, I was having my own troubles, as will appear later. And Lionel had established himself as a lady's man quite outside the context of my father's plans for his children's marriage; he took the line of least resistance and had affairs when he felt like it, going as far as opportunity allowed. There was no question of marriage, of course; he was just enjoying himself. How I used to envy him, with his free and easy way with girls and his ability to charm them at will! This was, of course, a secret life as far as my parents were concerned. No matter of principle or lack of principle was involved—unlike Sylvia and me Lionel did not make matters of principle out of this side of his life (though I must state in all honesty that it was timidity rather than moral principle that prevented me from becoming a Don Juan as a youngster). He was simply sowing his wild oats cheerfully and unself-consciously. Nor was there any question of his defying family tradition. In all overt matters he respected that tradition; in many ways, as time was to show, he was more bound up with it than any of us. But he exhibited at this time a streak of unreflective opportunism, which, together with his great natural charm, gave him an unfair advantage. I remember when I was in my last year at school and Lionel was at the university, how completely I accepted his superiority when it came to captivating a girl. I was both highly romantic and deeply frustrated—an unfortunate and uncomfortable mixture—and would make timid and self-conscious approaches to girls at parties; but if Lionel claimed one in whom I felt some interest I resigned her to him at once. I refused to compete. Later, when I was at the university, I made my own friends and learned to handle these matters in my own way. Looking back now, it is not difficult to present the balance sheet. Lionel had the gayer time and conquered far more girls; but mine, in the long run, was incalculably the deeper and happier experience.

I have talked up till now as though there were only three of us children—Lionel, Sylvia, and myself. And so there were, for a long time. But when Sylvia was nearly nine and I was nearly eleven-and-a-half and Lionel almost thirteen, our sister Beryl was born, the baby of the family. She was far enough behind to seem to us of a different generation. Sylvia was maternal to her; Lionel and I were avuncular. We never thought of ourselves as four children, but as the usual three, and then Beryl. Lionel and I treated her as a sort of mascot. We raced her pram down Blackford Hill, took her scrambling over Arthur's Seat, read stories to her, fed her with fantastic information which she eagerly lapped up. When I was working for my Higher Leaving Certificate I would do my chemistry revision aloud, and she would pick up odd facts, such as the valency of sulphur in sulphur trioxide. This encouraged me to feed her deliberately with facts and figures of this sort, which she memorized without, of course, understanding. She would astound visitors by reciting complicated chemical equations at the age of five. At the age of seven she had to write a little story about King Alfred and the cakes for school: I was then taking the British history class at the university, and I dictated to her a long disquisition about the historicity of the story and the origin of the legend, which she duly wrote down in her notebook and presented to the astonished teacher. We had immense fun with her—at least Lionel and I did. Sylvia was devoted to her in a more purely maternal way, looked after her whenever our mother was ill or busy, protected her with jealous efficiency. My father delighted in her; he would relax more in playing with her than at any other time.

As far as Jewish matters went, I have the impression now that Beryl was from the beginning further away from the older tradition than the rest of us. Not that there was any visible difference in the Jewish atmosphere of our home when she was a child; the same rituals, the same festivals, the same observances. But, though Beryl was naturally taught Hebrew, I don't think she was drilled in Jewish matters the way we were; and there were all sorts of little freedoms which Lionel, Sylvia, and I had bit by bit wrested from our parents which she grew up to take completely for granted. She participated more fully in school life than the rest of us ever did, and she relaxed her strict observance of the Sabbath at an earlier age and, I should imagine, with less inward argument than the rest of us. She was more like Lionel than like Sylvia and me in that respect, though not at all like him in others. She was still at school when war broke out in 1939. The rest of us had all left the family home by then, and it was a lonely life for her. My mother had bouts of serious illness during the war, and Beryl had to manage the house as well as do her school and later her university work. No wonder that she was pining to get away, to join one of the uniformed services and do something for the war effort. She did so as soon as she could, taking the abbreviated wartime university course (though she did not have to, as a potential teacher) and joining the W.A.A.F. I saw her in November, 1944, for the first time since September, 1939. I was home on a brief leave from my war job in Washington and Beryl got leave from the R.A.F. station where she was posted to come to see me. I had left her a schoolgirl with pigtails, a lively, romping, playful, altogether delightful child. The young lady in W.A.A.F. uniform who came in the front door to greet me on that November night was at first a complete stranger. I was shocked and desolated to find the schoolgirl I remembered so well completely lost in the uniformed, hearty young woman before me. I was able to find traces of the lost girl in her later, but never completely. She was grown up now and, it seemed, of a wholly different generation.

I suppose it was partly the war and the conditions of life in a uniformed service that helped Beryl to cast off all Jewish religious observance with such casual indifference that she did not even seem to take notice that she was doing it. She was still in the W.A.A.F. when my father died and when after the war she came back to teach for a while in Edinburgh, living with Mother, she made no attempt to conceal her utter indifference to the Jewish observance which we were brought up to practice. The rest of us at least kept things up when we were at home in Edinburgh, but Beryl had Sylvia's hatred of hypocrisy and refused on principle to observe customs that had no meaning for her. She had moved in the same direction as I for one had, but much more quickly and with apparently no sentimental memories of Jewish family life in the days of our childhood. I think that in the light of her wartime experiences, alone with her preoccupied parents in a grimly "utility" wartime Edinburgh, she had come to associate all Jewish observance with restriction and dreariness. Will she agree when she reads this? Will she be surprised or annoyed? I don't know. She was always a gay girl, full of life and spirits, much sought after, much admired. She is excellent company, efficient, humorous, self-possessed. Am I blaming her for having put the past behind her too easily, when I did it only after so much mental agony? Perhaps the truth is that I cannot forgive her for growing up.

CHAPTER 7

The morning slow train from Edinburgh to Dundee used to stop (as I suppose it still does) at many of the Fife coast towns on the way. This is why the train used to be, in the 1920's, the favorite mode of transport of those Edinburgh Jews who made a precarious living as itinerant salesmen, peddling anything from sewing needles to ready-made dresses among the good housewives and fisherfolk of Fife. They were the "trebblers," in their own Scots-Yiddish idiom; they had come as young men from Lithuania or Poland seeking freedom and opportunity but somehow had never got on as they had planned. Those with more push and enterprise had moved westward to Glasgow and often on from there to America; a few had managed to build up flourishing businesses in Edinburgh; but the trebblers were the failures, who spent their days carrying their battered suitcases from door to door in the little gray towns of Fife, to return home in the evening, with a pound or so gained, to a shabby but comfortable flat in one of the more run-down districts of Edinburgh. There, in old stone buildings where the gentry and nobility of Scotland had lived in the eighteenth and early nineteenth centuries, within a stone's throw of the "Royal Mile" with its violent and picturesque historical associations, they re-created the atmosphere of the ghetto and lived a life of self-contained Jewish orthodoxy.

Edinburgh, one of the few European capitals with no anti-Semitism in its history, accepted them with characteristic cool interest. In its semislums they learned such English as they knew, which meant in fact that they grafted the debased Scots of the Edinburgh streets onto their native Yiddish to produce one of the most remarkable dialects ever spoken by man. (Yet not such a comically incredible speech as my American friends seem to imagine: Scots preserves many Germanic words lost in standard English and found, in a similar or even identical form, in Yiddish, such as "lift" for air (German *luft*), "licht" for light (identical in Scots, German, and Yiddish), "hoast" for cough (German *husten*). Douglas Young has pointed out that Goethe's last words, *"mehr Licht,"* would have been pronounced the same in Scots, "mair licht"; and they would be the same in Yiddish.) Their sons and daughters, making full use of the city's admirable educational facilities, grew up to be doctors and scientists and professors, changing their names from Pinkinsky to Penn, from Finkelstein to Fenton, from Turiansky to Torrence. But they themselves, the Scottish-Jewish pioneers who never quite got where they wanted to go, changed nothing. On Fridays in the winter, when the sun set early, they would be home by the middle of the afternoon, to welcome the Sabbath. On Saturdays, of course, as well as on all Jewish festivals, there was no trebbling. And on weekdays in the Dundee train they would chant their morning prayers, strapping their phylacteries onto arm and forehead.

It was a strange thing to see, a compartment full of trebblers at their morning prayers. They were rarely inter-

[151]

rupted by gentiles. They had perfected a technique for getting compartments to themselves, and even if they had not, it would have taken a hardy outsider to enter a compartment where a swaying, bearded figure stood chanting at the window. Old Moishe Pinkinsky, a huge round-shouldered man with a red beard and a peculiar fierceness of gesticulation (which belied the essential gentleness of his nature), scared off many a would-be interloper. Once, however, when the train was particularly crowded, a desperate latecomer did succeed in entering the compartment occupied by Moishe and his companions. He sat in astonished silence while the trebblers concluded their devotions, and then listened, bewildered, as they talked to each other in Yiddish. But Moishe had a kind heart, and he felt sorry for this lost soul sitting opposite him. He took down a brown paper parcel from the rack and extracted from it a huge sandwich of black bread and chopped herring. This he broke in two, and keeping half for himself he handed the other half to the fearful gentile. "Nem!" ("Take!") he said kindly. The man's name was Mackenzie, and he was an insurance agent on his way to Burntisland: he later told the story to his friends in an Edinburgh bar. "I ate for dear life," he said. "And, you know, it tasted damn good. Some kind of caviar."

The anecdote I have just told was part of the Edinburgh Jewish folklore which grew up in the city in the first quarter of this century. I cannot vouch for its literal truth, any more than I can for the effectiveness of the trebblers' devotions in scaring away non-Jewish passengers. But these stories are all probable in the Aristotelian sense. I myself, on the one occasion when I went to Dundee on that train, saw the trebblers in their special compartments, a voluntary and jealously preserved segregation. Recently

[152]

I received a letter from the son of the man who was station-master at one of the small railway stations where the earliest trebblers would alight; he told me how, at the very beginning of this century, these Jewish immigrants, not yet knowing any English, would converse with his father, they talking in Yiddish and he in broad Scots, with perfectly adequate mutual intelligibility. Scots-Yiddish as a working language must have been developing rapidly in the years immediately preceding World War I. It must have been one of the most short-lived languages in the world. I should guess that 1912 to 1940 was the period of its flourishing. The younger generation, who grew up in the 1920's and 1930's, of course did not speak it, though they knew Yiddish; and while there is an occasional old man in Edinburgh who speaks it today, one has to seek it out in order to find it, and in another decade it will be gone forever. "Aye man, ich hob' getrebbelt mit de five o'clock train," one trebbler would say to another. "Vot time's yer *bar mitzvie*, laddie?" I was once asked. "Ye'll hae a drap o' bramfen (whisky)? It's Dzon Beck. Ye ken: 'Nem a schmeck fun Dzon Beck.' " ("Take a peg of John Begg," the advertising slogan of John Begg whisky.)

There was one word in the Scots-Yiddish vocabulary that has always puzzled me: this was "bleggage," applied to an ill-behaved youngster. My father used to maintain that it was a corruption of "blackguard," and perhaps it was a mixture of "blackguard" and "baggage." Whatever its origin, it was a fine, expressive word, and it was never more effectively used than one Sabbath morning in 1919 when a number of enterprising youngsters had climbed onto the roof of the Graham Street synagogue and were making a noise on the skylight. The chazan (cantor) stopped his singing, banged his large prayer book with the flat of his

hand, and cried out: "Shah! Mak a quietness! *Bleggages!*"
This was just after my father had accepted his appoint-
ment as Edinburgh rabbi, and the incident was symbolic
of the kind of chaos he was determined to put a stop to.

We ourselves had little contact with what might be
called the trebbling stratum of Edinburgh Jews. We met
them in shul and saw them often enough in the streets of
the city or at Waverley Station, and we exchanged Scottish-Jewish funny stories with their children, but my father's view of the nature of a Scottish-Jewish community
and its future development as a separate but equal part of
the culture within which it lived left little room for these
people. He got on well with them, and looked after their
religious needs, acting with respect to them much more
like the old-fashioned "rebbe" than like the spiritual
leader of Scottish Jewry, a public figure with a dignified
part to play in Scotland's capital, which was his most impressive role. The trebblers combined Jewish orthodoxy
with superstition and were unable to distinguish between
central Jewish traditions and the flimsiest kind of folklore. ("Shah! Iz nit mazel" ["Be quiet! It's unlucky!"], one
of the most patriarchal of the trebblers said angrily to his
wife when she started to offer me her condolences on the
death of my father.) Moishe Pinkinsky could be of no help
to my father in his ambition to reconcile rabbinic Judaism
with Western secular culture. Moishe and his like were regarded in our family with affectionate indulgence as interesting examples of a transitional stage in the emancipation
from the ghetto.

I think now that they had more to offer than our aristocratic family attitude conceded. They had a folk wisdom
of their own, and a tremendous emotional vitality in their
way of living. I remember Motty Rifkind, a shambling,

[154]

grizzled man, the elder and the more uncouth of two extremely pious brothers. He sat next to me once in shul one Passover morning, and was indignant with some young men, infrequent visitors to the synagogue, who were chattering loudly throughout the chazan's repetition of the *Amidah* (an important prayer, with "eighteen benedictions," which the congregation recite first, standing, and then the chazan repeats). As old Motty himself used the synagogue as if it were his club, sleeping, snoring, talking, arguing, or praying as the spirit moved him, I was a little surprised at his stern view of the talkers, and indicated as much. In reply he told me a story. "Two men," he said, "vent into a poob and ordered a gless beer. Dey hadna been in dat poob more dan vonce or tvice before. Vell, dey sip deir beer un' dey sit talking un' *shmoosing* [chatting]. Dey sit un' talk un' talk. At lest de barman leans over de counter und he says to dem: 'Drink op yer beer. Get oot frae here. Ye coom into ma poob vonce a year un' ye tink ye can sit here un' *shmoos* for hours as do' ye owned de place. Ma regular customers can sit un' talk over deir beer as long as dey like. But no' you. Oot!' *Nu,* dat's hoo it is mit a shul. I come here every veek und *Hakodosh boruch hu* ["the Holy One, blessed be He," that is, God] kens me vell, un' he don't mind if I take it easy. But dess bleggages, dat come vonce or tvice a year—no! Dey daven [pray] or dey shot op."

Another remarkable character, who spoke Scots-Yiddish though he was no trebbler, was the *shamosh* or beadle of the synagogue, a ginger-bearded gentleman called Rubenstein, who had an extraordinary number of talents. He used to teach the elementary class in the cheder, and an extraordinarily effective teacher he was, too, though his methods would have horrified any modern educationist. He taught

[155]

everything by simple repetition; the class would chant the words together over and over again in a sleepy, monotonous singsong, until they knew them. I remember on summer evenings hearing the Hebrew chanting float out of the open windows of Sciennes School, a handsome gray stone public elementary school that stood at the top of our street, and wondering what the passers-by would think. (Incidentally, the fact that the cheder was conducted in one of the Edinburgh Education Authority's schools and no longer in the damp basement of the Graham Street synagogue was a characteristic achievement of my father's. He proved to the Edinburgh Corporation, or whoever was responsible, that the teaching of Hebrew to Jewish children in Edinburgh was an integral part of the city's educational activities, with the result that this school was put at his service, after ordinary school hours, free, and the cheder was able to move from its cramped and inadequate basement quarters.) Rubenstein was extremely well up on Jewish customs and traditions, he knew to a nicety how to vary the tune of the chanting on the different holy days and at precisely what angle the feet should be kept while standing up to pray (the posture was modeled on the description of the angels praying in the book of Ezekiel), so that, although he had a voice that croaked like a raven's, he often acted as *chazan sheini* or second cantor. He also was in charge of a boys' service on Sunday mornings, where a different boy conducted the proceedings each week and so everyone learned the rather tricky process. Though my father sent Lionel and me to Rubenstein's service, for he felt we ought to know how to conduct a weekday service (something that every Jew is supposed to be able to do and may be called on to do as a mark of honor or sympathy), he was not very happy about it. He wanted us to learn all our

[156]

religious and Hebrew knowledge from him rather than from a character, however estimable, who had only half emerged from the ghetto.

The living that Rubenstein made from his activities as *shamosh*, Hebrew teacher, and extra cantor, he found far from adequate, and to eke out his income he engaged in a remarkable number of private enterprises. He would sell you anything. He specialized in obtaining articles required for Jewish worship, and he sold not only prayer books and praying shawls but Palestine wine and brandy and the palm branches and citrons used at the Feast of Tabernacles. He had no license to sell wines and spirits and his activities here were completely illegal; but nobody worried about that. Even my father, one of the most scrupulous men in the world where the law was concerned, would not hesitate to send me to Rubenstein's house to ask for a bottle of "oil," which was delivered wrapped up in layers of brown paper and marked "frying oil" on the outside. Rubenstein made a fair amount of money out of his various activities and eventually bought himself a handsome house in a residential area of the city. It was after he had moved there that he formed the habit of dropping in at a pub in Dalkeith Road for a small whisky or two. With his neatly trimmed beard and dignified bearing, he was taken by the barmaid and by the habitués of the pub for the rabbi, and I remember how horrified my father was when he learned this, especially at the detail that a certain brand of whisky had become known in this pub as the "rabbi's choice."

Rubenstein was something of a tippler, but only once a year did he get really drunk, and I have never seen a man set about it with more deliberation and dignity. It was on Simchas Torah, the Feast of the Rejoicing of the Law, when one is supposed to have a merry time, that he would engage on his annual spree. There would always be a modest feast prepared in the synagogue hall after the morning service on Simchas Torah; glasses of wine for the young people and ladies, whisky for the maturer males, and biscuits. My father would stay to make kiddush (sanctification; that is, ask a blessing) over the wine, and then leave; but Lionel and I would linger on to watch Rubenstein tanking up and to see what was going to happen. The climax was well worth waiting for. People would keep pressing glasses of whisky on him, and as he knocked them back in rapid succession (he had the extraordinary faculty, which I have seen in no one else, of being able to throw drink right down his gullet without any contraction of muscles for swallowing) his face would begin to glow redder and redder, and at length he would begin to address the company in Yiddish, making what was evidently an extremely funny speech of which I could never make out more than a few words. Then someone would clear a path between the glasses on the long trestle table: this was the signal for the grand finale. Up jumped Rubenstein onto the table and, singing a song punctuated with frequent shouts and "oi's," he moved down the table in a species of cossack dance, arms folded, knees bent, legs kicked out alternately. Never once did he knock over a glass. The whisky seemed to give him a curious kind of stability and control: the whole performance appeared to me superhuman. Up the long table he danced, then turned and danced back, singing and shouting, while the spectators clapped rhythmically. Then he jumped down, and the party was over. Lionel and I would hurry home, to be scolded for being late for dinner.

When I last saw Rubenstein, not long ago, he was verging on eighty, but looked as trim and spry as ever. My

[158]

father, he told me, had worked too hard, and that had been
the cause of his death. We were both silent for a moment
and then he laughed and said: "I never vork too hard.
Dat's vy I keep so vell. Vonce dey asked me to take an extra
class at cheder. But I vasna having any. 'Nae bloody fear,'
I said."

Scots-Yiddish was the language of those immigrant Edinburgh Jews who for the most part never managed to rise
very high in the social or financial scale. It must not be
confused with the more courtly though equally quaint broken English spoken by well-to-do immigrants who pros-
pered in business. Notable among these (or perhaps he was
really unique and I am constructing a class out of a single
individual) was Mr. Solomon Sklovsky, a somewhat deaf
old man with a beautifully clean white beard and a fresh
rosy face, who had made a fortune out of sugar. He had the
reputation of complete probity combined with extreme
cunning in the business world, and many stories were told
of his shrewdness and enterprise. Thrift for him was the
greatest of virtues ("Trift," he called it), and whenever an
Edinburgh Jewish boy celebrated his *bar mitzvah* he
would open an account for him at the savings bank with a
deposit of one pound. He was not fundamentally unchari-
table by disposition, but he had to be persuaded of the
complete worthiness of any cause before he would give a
penny to it, and many a weary evening my father spent
wrestling with him before extracting a promise to give a
substantial sum to some Jewish or general charity. I think
he enjoyed having to be persuaded, and was particularly
pleased when a complete delegation waited on him; it
gave him a sense of his own importance. He knew, too,
that everyone waited to see how much Solomon Sklovsky
("Shlomo," he was called, the Hebrew for "Solomon," and

this became corrupted somehow to "Shlabber") would give before deciding on his own contribution.

Old Shlabber lived in a world by himself. He was a widower when I first knew him, living alone with, I believe, a housekeeper of some sort to look after him. At the synagogue he would sit nodding his head and stroking his snowy beard, occasionally turning to his neighbor to roar out some observation or question. His deafness made him imagine that everyone else had to be shouted at, and once he startled me by roaring at me across several empty seats, during the Reading of the Law one Sabbath morning: "De Hebrew lankvitch is de FINEST lankvitch in de vorlt." He professed to scorn the younger businessmen who were coming to the fore in community affairs, and on one occasion, when the newly elected *parness* and *gabai* (president and treasurer) of the congregation took their seats for the first time in the special box appointed for them in the synagogue, he was heard muttering to himself as he eyed them: "Fonny tink. VERY fonny tink." His appearance was incredibly venerable; he was by far the most patriarchal looking of all the Edinburgh Jews. When, early in 1925, my father left from Waverley Station, Edinburgh, to go to Palestine for the opening of the Hebrew University in Jerusalem, Shlabber Sklovsky was among the group of senior members of his congregation who came to see him off. A photographer from one of the Edinburgh evening papers took a photograph of the scene, and that evening a picture of Shlabber appeared, with the caption: "Dr. Salis Daiches, Chief Rabbi [my father was often called Chief Rabbi though he had no such official title and always disclaimed it when it was given him], leaving Waverley Station, Edinburgh, on his way to Jerusalem for the opening of the Hebrew University." Obviously, the subeditor or whoever it was who handled this item assumed that this venerable, patriarchal figure must be the rabbi, and cut out the rest of the photograph. My mother was most distressed when she saw this, and communicated with the newspaper, with the result that the next day a proper photograph of my father appeared, with a similar caption. But the damage had been done: my mother received some days later a puzzled letter from an old Liverpool friend whom she had not seen since the early years of her marriage, saying that she had seen the photograph of my father in the paper and she was upset to find how much he had aged, and indeed changed beyond recognition.

Shlabber's pronunciation of English was something quite original, and when combined with his characteristic roar made his speech unmistakable. I remember once answering the telephone when my father was out, with the ensuing conversation going something like this:

MYSELF: Hello?

SHLABBER (*roaring*): Goot eefning, Doctor Daiches!

MYSELF: I'm sorry, Mr. Sklovsky, but Dr. Daiches isn't in.

SHLABBER: HA?

MYSELF: I'm sorry, Mr. Sklovsky, but Dr. Daiches isn't in.

SHLABBER: HA??

MYSELF: (*shouting*): I'm sorry, Mr. Sklovsky, but Dr. Daiches isn't in.

SHLABBER (*roaring even louder than before, in a tone of absolute astonishment*): HOW DID YOU KNOW IT VOSS ME?

To the younger generation, these picturesque older men were the object of affectionate amusement. Some of the younger businessmen, born and bred in Edinburgh, were sometimes embarrassed when some of the more eccentric older characters appeared in the midst of a conversation with a non-Jewish colleague or customer. On one occasion, when a young Jewish rug-dealer in Edinburgh was interrupted in a talk with a titled Scottish customer by two bearded, Yiddish-speaking collectors for a Jewish charity (one of them a bandy-legged redheaded man of incredibly slovenly appearance, who always wore, indoors and out, a too large bowler hat perched on the back of his head), he got rid of the intruders rapidly and then lightly remarked to the customer: "Those are the Persians from whom I buy my rugs." But on the whole there was little friction between different elements in the Jewish community or between the Jewish community and its non-Jewish neighbors. My father's success in welding the community into a single unit worshiping in the same synagogue had a great deal to do with this, while the Scottish Presbyterians' natural interest in the People of the Book helped to maintain good relations between Jews and Christians. Edinburgh University, for example, never made any difficulty about changing the dates of examinations when my father pointed out that they fell on Jewish festivals and Jewish students would therefore be unable to take them; and on one occasion, when I was the only Jewish candidate, the professor sent the question paper to my father and asked him to see that I took the exam under the proper conditions. (My father stood outside the drawing-room door with his watch in his hand, and I never had to hand in a paper so punctually on the stroke of the hour as I had to on that occasion.) And before the war, when many Jewish students in America were finding it difficult to enter medical schools, my father arranged with the University of Edinburgh (and I think, but I am not positive, with the Royal College of Surgeons at Edinburgh as well) for the admission of a high proportion of American Jewish students for that reason. There must be hundreds of Jewish doctors in America now who, though they have never realized it, owe their medical degree to the fact that my father intervened with the appropriate authorities to have them and their fellow citizens admitted at one or other of the two Edinburgh medical schools.

There are many other older Jewish characters who come to mind as I think of my childhood in Edinburgh. There is little Mr. Lurie, who sat next to me in shul, who still greets me when I come back to Edinburgh and revisit the familiar synagogue with: *"Sholom aleichem* ("Peace be with you"). Vell Davie, howyer keepin'?" "Howyer keepin'?," spoken in a peculiarly clipped accent, is the special way of greeting someone after long absence among these older Edinburgh Jews. Sometimes it is varied with, "Keepin' alright?" with a strong, upswinging interrogative inflection on the "alright" (and sometimes an indeterminate vowel creeps its way in between the "all" and the "right"). There was Mr. Solstone the tailor, dead many years now, whose beautiful new car (or was it his son's?) rolled backward and fell over what he persisted in calling "de barrication" beside Peebles Hydro. And I must not close these reminiscences without some mention of Yudel Simenoff, a man who combined extreme Jewish piety with Marxist learning and who, by reason of some palatal defect, was unable to speak his Scots-Yiddish dialect (for he, too, was one of the trebblers) without a whole battery of incidental spluttering noises. There were not more than half a dozen people in Edinburgh, outside his immediate family, who could understand him, and when he arose, as he unfail-

[163]

ingly did, to make some remarks during the question period that followed the weekly lecture at the Edinburgh Jewish Literary Society, there were few if any who understood what he was talking about. Through hearing him often enough, I finally learned to understand him, and found to my surprise that he was in his way a learned and intelligent man, who knew a considerable amount about both Jewish folklore and folk song (his speech defect disappeared when he sang) and modern economics. In later life he began to write letters to the Edinburgh evening papers on economic and political affairs, and his opinions aroused respectful interest in many quarters. This was some twenty years ago, and when I was in Edinburgh soon after the war ended I did not expect to see him still flourishing. But I found that he had been discovered by the folklorists and had just been engaged to make some recordings of Jewish folk song and liturgical chants for the B.B.C. I realized then that somebody should have recorded the speech of Motty Rifkind and Moishe Pinkinsky in the 1920's and 1930's, the golden years of Scots-Yiddish. But nobody had thought of it then, and it was too late now.

The native-born Edinburgh Jews were rather proud of these older picturesque characters, and the community has become less colorful now that they have almost all gone. Those of my own generation exchange stories about them with nostalgic affection, and many of them wrote me of their pleasure when the substance of what I have written here first appeared in a separate article. A few, however, were resentful. They, significantly, belonged to the older generation of native born, the first generation to establish themselves as original English-speaking citizens of Edinburgh. This group had always been particularly nervous of what the mass of non-Jewish citizenry would think. "A shame and disgrace for the neighbors" was a common phrase among them if any Edinburgh Jew did something outside the pattern of ordinary middle-class respectability. Some of them were so anxious not to offend that they developed somewhat curious notions of what was respectable and what was not. "Bad taste," remarked one of these gentlemen to my uncle, making a wry face, on reading my article. A shame and disgrace for the neighbors, in fact. But the neighbors didn't think so.

CHAPTER 8

My brother Lionel and I slept, throughout most of our childhood, in a large sparsely furnished room at the top of our three-story house. It looked out across our own back garden to the back greens of the flats in Livingstone Place, where we could see housewives hanging up the clothes on washing day or at their windows, working by the sink. My bed was nearer the window, and it was my duty to open the window both top and bottom before settling down for the night. We both believed in fresh air, and the thought of sleeping with the windows shut—even in the dead of winter, and in an unheated room—would have horrified us. My father, however, had more old-fashioned notions on these matters. Every night, before going to bed himself, he would come up to our bedroom to make sure that all was well; he would close the bottom part of the window and pull out two of the three sections of shutter which were always built in (on the inside of the window) to serve as alternatives or supplements to blinds in older Edinburgh houses: the third, middle, section was hinged onto one of the other sections and folded behind it when the shutters were put back. Lionel and I would argue strenuously with our father about the question of window shutting; we insisted that we should suffocate if the bottom part of the window were closed, and my father protested that we would catch cold if it were left open. He had originally wanted to close both top and bottom and pull out all the shutters as well, but he reluctantly agreed to compromise by closing only the bottom window and leaving the middle section of shutter open, and eventually we allowed him to do this, though we kept on murmuring. We had our own way, at any rate, between the time of our going to bed and the time, generally a couple of hours later, when my father came up on his nightly visitation before going to bed himself. Sometimes, if Lionel or I woke up after my father had paid his nightly visit, the bottom of the window would be reopened and the shutters folded back into the wall.

Neither of us had a bedside lamp, and the last one into bed had to pad across the cold linoleum to switch off the light by the door and then cross the room again in the dark. One winter Lionel, who was more enterprising than I was at that sort of thing, rigged up a complicated system of strings and pulleys which would enable either of us to put on or turn off the light without getting out of bed. It was fairly easy to rig up something which would switch the light on, but turning it off—which meant putting the switch *up,* and the switch was fairly high up on the wall— was a complicated matter to arrange, if it was to be done from a prone position. However, Lionel managed it, and the bedroom became a maze of strings running both horizontally and vertically. When my father came up the attic stairs that night to see that all was well and close the bottom part of the window, he ran inadvertently into this complicated machinery. He soon realized what it was for, and found to his dismay that he had dislocated an important part of the device so that the light could no longer be turned off from my bed. I was awake—I think the noise of his stumbling into the strings must have awakened me— and lay quietly watching. I thought he would have dismissed the whole thing as a silly prank, but to my surprise he looked genuinely distressed at finding that he had damaged the apparatus and immediately set about trying to repair it. My father was not deft with his fingers, and soon found himself in difficulties. He got down on the floor, he stretched toward the ceiling, he fiddled about with ends of strings, only to dislocate the machinery still further. Then he decided to remove all the strings and begin again from the beginning, working the thing out from first principles. Obviously, he didn't want us to be disappointed when we woke up in the morning. A rush of affection came over me as I watched him trying so hard and so vainly to restore the damage, and at last I could bear it no longer but jumped out of bed, exclaiming: "It's all right. Don't bother. I can sort it." ("Sort" is the common Edinburgh word for "mend" or "fix.") My father watched rather sheepishly as I restored the apparatus to its original preposterous form, and then said: "You'll catch cold. And why are you awake at this time of night?" There was no real reproof in his words, which were meant kindly, an attempt to establish communication. Indeed, his journey up to the top floor of the house each night before going to bed was itself a kindly and even sentimental gesture. But, though his life was full of such gestures, he found it difficult to put them spontaneously and informally into words. The most eloquent of men on formal, public occasions, he nevertheless found it hard to establish completely relaxed verbal communication with his children.

I fancy that he was like that, though in less degree, with

[168]

my mother too. I remember once, for her birthday, he bought her a handbag more expensive than he could afford and handed it to her with an extraordinarily gauche gesture. Neither he nor my mother knew what to say on the occasion: he was scolded for his extravagance. Years later, when I read Virginia Woolf's *Mrs. Dalloway* and came across the incident where Richard Dalloway brings flowers home to his wife because he cannot find words to express what he wants to say, I thought I recognized the situation:

"But he wanted to come in holding something. Flowers? Yes, flowers . . . The time comes when it can't be said; one's too shy to say it. . . . Here he was walking across London to say to Clarissa in so many words that he loved her. Which one never does say, he thought. Partly one's lazy; partly one's shy. . . ."

It was not laziness on my father's part, but a certain kind of shyness which seemed to overcome him in the simpler and more intimate affairs of life. Not that he lacked a robust sense of humor, or was incapable of joking with his family. He would listen tolerantly when Lionel or I vented our schoolboy humor at the dinner table, and would thoroughly enjoy our imitations of some of the more eccentric or picturesque members of his congregation. He was never in the least distressed when we engaged in somewhat boisterous fun during the Seder night at the beginning of Passover, or when, on one occasion, I read to the assembled family and guests after the Seder was over a would-be humorous parody of the service followed by a mystery story about a dubious Jewish preacher entitled "Muffled in Matzo-meal, or the Mystery of the Meshugga Maggid [*i.e.*, of the Mad Preacher]." He had his own favorite jokes, too, and he would tell them with a roar of

[169]

laughter which would sometimes go on until tears of mirth trickled down his cheeks and he was gasping for breath. I don't think I have ever known anybody with such a hearty laugh. He had also a somewhat academic fondness for the pun, and he would often make a punning remark at dinner and then look round the table with a smile for approval. (When he found grounds in his black coffee after dinner, he would look up and say, "Grounds for complaint." He must have made this remark a score of times, yet each time he expected the same approval.) But he was incapable of talking cheerfully affectionate nonsense to his family. His affection for and pride in us all was intense, but he could not express it easily in the give and take of daily conversation. When angered he could thunder at us most eloquently (we simply kept quiet and waited till the storm passed over), but mostly his talk was rather deliberate, rather formal.

I have, however, some very dim recollections of myself sitting on my father's knee as a very small child and being joggled up and down to the accompaniment of some nonsense verse (I seem to recall the phrase "jingle-jangle-jorum") or of the verse:

> Sandy Still belongs to the mill
> And the mill belongs to Sandy still;
> Sandy Still belongs to the mill
> And the mill belongs to Sandy.

And once, in the pocket of a very old dress coat of my father's that was brought forth from the dark recesses of some cupboard in a vast spring cleaning, we found a pair of white gloves (ladies'?) and a printed set of comic verses composed by him for his brother's wedding in (I think) 1905. The theme of the verses was the startling change about to take place in the state of both bride and groom: the chorus was the Latin tag, *"O quae mutatio rerum."*

When Lionel and I were students at Edinburgh University and would occasionally bring home a fellow student for tea, he would converse with him with a grave, old-world courtesy, always very punctilious about calling him *Mister* So-and-so, perhaps cracking a carefully prepared joke, talking about current affairs as though to an equal. Our university friends (who were mostly non-Jewish) were pleased and flattered by his manner and enjoyed talking with him. It is true that he occasionally got them mixed up, and was liable to say to Mr. X, who was studying law, "And you are the brilliant history student, aren't you?"—thinking of Mr. Y, who had been to tea a few weeks before. But nobody seemed to mind that. And when he did learn what the student's main interest was, he would set out to make deliberate conversation on that topic. Once, I remember, he took a philosophy student into his study to chat with him about David Hume and Kant, and left me waiting outside, saying to myself ruefully that after all the visitor was *my* friend and had come to see *me*. The young man emerged thoroughly charmed.

My father never expected either Lionel or me to follow in his footsteps and take up the rabbinical profession, in spite of the fact that we came from a long line of rabbis stretching far back into the early Middle Ages and beyond, and we would be the first generation to break that tradition. It was clear from the beginning that Lionel had no ambitions that way; I went through a phase when I thought I should like to be a rabbi, but was very properly not taken seriously. Law was the subject my father's mind turned to when thinking of his sons' future. There is something about law which has always attracted the rabbinical mind, and my father himself, trained on Talmudic argument, had considerable legal ability. My uncle, a rabbi and a distinguished Biblical scholar and teacher of rabbinics in London, read law for amusement in his spare time and was called to the bar, though he hardly ever practiced. So law was established in our family as a thoroughly suitable profession for a member of a rabbinical family. For Lionel, it was the obvious and proper choice; he had exactly the qualities of mind to make a good barrister (or advocate, as we say in Scotland). My own literary bent showed itself early, and I had no doubt myself of what I wanted to be. My father, though never discouraging my literary ambitions, at first assumed that I would want to go on and take a law degree after getting my honors degree in English at Edinburgh University. Literature, he thought, was an excellent thing as a second string. His attitude, in fact, was so similar to that of Robert Louis Stevenson's father to *his* son's literary ambitions (and, for that matter, to Walter Scott's father's attitude to his) that when I first read the life of Stevenson I was struck by the coincidence. (Indeed, the similarities between Stevenson's life and my own have often struck me since. Stevenson's problems as a young man in Edinburgh were startlingly like my own; his relations with his father were like mine; we both went to America for similar reasons; we both achieved the same kind of ultimate reconciliation with our families.) When I resisted the suggestion that I should proceed to a law degree after completing my degree in English, my father never brought the matter up again. I think he was impressed by my own confidence that I could make my way successfully in the literary profession. Most of the discussions on my career took place during my last year at school. When I entered the university and demonstrated

[172]

how easy I found it to win distinction in literary courses, my father (who had not, I suspect, realized the possibilities of an academic career in literature before) seemed perfectly happy to let me go my own way. He boasted of my successes to his friends; and when I was elected Fellow of Balliol College, Oxford, he saw to it that the news was in the Edinburgh papers.

Life for my father had its duties and its courtesies, which he observed with what I can only call a scrupulous innocence. The subtleties of personal intercourse were left unspoken. It was the same with his attitude to religion. We all had our duties, which we were expected to fulfill. We had to learn our Hebrew, attend shul regularly, wash our hands before eating and say grace afterward, and (it went without saying) refrain from any of the activities offensive to an enlightened Jewish orthodoxy. Lionel and I would argue with our father about the reason for this or that Jewish observance, or even question its value or utility, but theology, or the mysteries of religion, or the nature of piety we never discussed with him. There was nothing of the mystic in my father, and his defense of Judaism (given often in addresses to literary societies and in articles in the press) was on the lines of a humanist utilitarianism: the good and useful and satisfying life was one led in accordance with laws and customs which safeguarded morality, preserved society, and decently canalized human instincts. The divine origin of such laws was a fact both manifested by Jewish history and required by human nature (for how could moral laws be absolute if they were not grounded in divine commands?). Yet his pulpit eloquence could reach to great emotional heights, and his magnificent sermons on Yom Kippur, the Day of Atonement, were full of deep religious feeling and a moving awareness of the ritual solemnity of communal repentance. I can see him now, rapt and prophetic in his white kittel, weak at the end of the day's fasting yet strong in voice and powerful in presence, leaning from the pulpit as he gives his final Yom Kippur sermon, his voice ringing out as he quotes and translates the Hebrew hymn beseeching forgiveness as the night falls and the day of penitence is coming to an end: "Open unto us the gate, at the time of the closing of the gate, for the day fadeth." I remember the *frisson* that used to go down my spine as I heard those words. Yet he would never take that tone in private conversation. It would have been unthinkable for him to talk to his family about sin or forgiveness or divine mercy. He would discuss with us the history of some law or custom, or the true meaning of some Biblical text, or the shortsightedness of the "Liberal" Jews in abandoning some traditional part of the liturgy or belittling the rabbinic tradition, but the ultimate truth of religion and the nature of religious experience were not for him topics of private conversation. After a day of religious exaltation and powerful preaching, he would return home on Yom Kippur night tired and relaxed to chat about the number of people in shul, decorum among the congregation, and the odd mumbling way in which old Mr. Sklovsky had read *maftir Yonah* (*i.e.*, the book of Jonah, which is read—or rather, chanted —by a distinguished member of the congregation at the conclusion of the afternoon Reading of the Law).

It may seem surprising that my father, who was so anxious to combine all that was best in modern thought with Jewish tradition and practice, should have been so opposed to Liberal Judaism (he himself rarely wrote that term without putting the first word in quotation marks), that modern Jewish movement whose aim is to concentrate on the finer ethical qualities of Judaism and prune away the element of tribal tabu (as they consider it) and rabbinical elaboration of minute prohibitions and observances. But in fact he was the implacable enemy of the movement. His synthesis combined orthodox, rabbinical Judaism with modern thought; to scrap every element of Jewish observance which modern thought would not accept was not to synthesize two different things but to tailor one to fit the other. And to tailor Judaism in that fashion meant substituting human claims to know what is good and right and to be able to distinguish the ethically valuable from the otiose for a belief in the divine origin of Jewish ethics. If the individual can go through the laws and practices which have developed in the course of Jewish tradition and say that some are still valuable and others are of no value and ought to be abandoned, then the individual is making himself the ultimate source of ethical absolutes, and saying that he will recognize as divine only what he, the individual, thinks is good. In his essay, "Progressive Judaism: An Analysis," which appeared in his book, *Aspects of Judaism,* he quoted C. G. Montefiore's statement: "Neither Hebrew Bible nor Rabbinic Talmud is immaculate or complete in doctrine or institution, in morality or in religion. We distinguish between the divine and human elements in both these books. . . . We distinguish doctrines and institutions which we desire to maintain for their truth and their value from doctrines and institutions which we desire to put aside or to abolish." And he commented: "So it is 'we,' i.e. the exponents of Liberal Judaism, who are in possession of the unerring standards of truth, morality, and religion, and the application of these standards to the doctrines and institutions of Bible and Talmud enables these independent thinkers

[175]

and moralists to decide for themselves what is true and what is false, what is valuable and what is valueless, what is permanent and what is transitory in the teaching and practices of Judaism." He went on to develop his argument against Liberal Judaism as follows:

The obvious question that must occur to the thoughtful reader of such a pronouncement is this: Whence do the founders of the new faith derive those definite standards of 'truth', 'morality', and 'religion?' If these are not to be found *in* the religious teachings, but are to be applied *to* them; if the contents of the Torah (Law) are to be valued in accordance with principles fixed *a priori* or brought to bear upon them from other spheres; and if the critic is to pronounce his verdict in accordance with the estimate derived from those principles, must it not be asked whence these principles have themselves been derived? From what source does the 'Liberal' or 'Progressive' Jew draw his 'Truth', his 'Morality', his 'Religion', and how are these principles conveyed from one man to another? How are they imparted from teacher to pupil, from preacher to congregation? If the source is known and accessible, can it not be indicated, so that all may be able to test its purity and reliability? If it is a secret, when and how and to whom has it been revealed? If any man can discover these principles by his own reasoning power and his own moral postulates, why not leave it to every one to evolve his own faith and to fix his own religious principles—if he at all needs such additional safeguards and motives for right conduct? . . .

Again and again my father stressed the principle that unless we believe in the divine origin of the Law, human society is in perpetual jeopardy. "There is scarcely an individual," he wrote in his essay "Modern Ethics and the Mosaic Law," "or a body of individuals, that does not feel entitled to take the law into his, or their, own hands when there is a chance of gaining some material advantage

[176]

or profit. Is it not likely, therefore, that under the influence of the existing tendency, with positive religion losing its hold upon modern society, lawlessness and licence will increase, and the climax will one day be reached in a new upheaval, the greatest *bellum omnium contra omnes* that ever existed in reality—until from the chaos a new order of things will develop and humanity will have learned a new great lesson." (This essay was written in the early 1920's.) Or again, even more explicitly: "If the command, 'Thou shalt love thy neighbour as thyself,' or 'Thou shalt not steal,' or 'Thou shalt not covet thy neighbour's house,' etc., comes from God, the creator of man, the source of all truth and righteousness, and the omniscient and omnipotent guide of man's destiny—then it *must* be effective, then it *must* be obeyed by us, however much in our own opinion its transgression would be justified. To be religious means, in the words of Kant, 'to recognize our duties as being divine commands.' But while with Kant 'divine commands' are nothing but dictates of man's own conscience, the average man will find that if the origin of those commands is not placed 'in the starred heaven above us,' his 'moral conscience' will soon enough leave him in the lurch. This is the lesson which the modern ethicist has yet to learn."

My father's chief objection to Liberal Judaism was thus that it made the individual conscience the arbiter of what was good and worth preserving and what was valueless and expendable in the Law which had come down to us as the Word of God. Once you take that view, divine authority is gone and chaos is come again. My father would defend the Word of God most persuasively in humanist terms; he would show how obedience to it was conducive to a rich and satisfying personal and community life and how it was compatible with the best that all moral philosophers have said; but he would admit no argument about the reality of its divine origin. Historical or anthropological arguments about the Bible never disturbed him in the least: this was all very well, he would say in effect, but you *must* believe in the divine origin of the Law if society is to flourish. Once, when I was in the throes of hammering out my own position in relation to my father's, I accused him in my thoughts of really taking up Voltaire's position: "If God did not exist it would be necessary to create him." But that was unfair; he had a profound religious sensibility beneath the philosophical and humanist surface, though he was not always able to make articulate use of it.

I discuss this in some detail, because it explains how my father unwittingly destroyed for me in advance any line of defense to which I might retreat when I came to doubt the literal divine inspiration of the Bible and the Talmudic tradition. The illogicality of the Liberal Jewish position was demonstrated for me once and for all. If the individual can pick and choose among the Biblical precepts, saying that some sound rather attractive and worth keeping while others seem primitive and superstitious, then obviously the individual is creating God in accordance with his own ideas and the objectivity of religion disappears. Any kind of "liberal" religion becomes a humane agnosticism using some of the forms of religion to find acceptance for its ethical views. It was a sad irony of fate that made my father's earnest and eloquent crusade against Liberal Judaism point the way to agnosticism for me; but in some sense that is what happened.

My father in his innocence took much for granted. Most of all, he took for granted that the deep, unmentioned roots of his own faith would spread automatically down the generations. He, as an orthodox Jewish rabbi and a student of Hume and Kant, had finally solved the relation between Judaism and modern secular culture and showed how one could be a free and equal citizen of a Western democracy while keeping up all orthodox Jewish observances: there was nothing for Lionel and me to do but to follow in his footsteps. Though he never thought of us as becoming rabbis, I don't think that it once crossed his mind that we would ever question his synthesis. And throughout our childhood the pattern of family loyalties and family affection was woven so closely and strongly that any such questioning was unthinkable. Even when as a child I wondered about the existence of God, it never occurred to me to wonder about my father's British-Jewish way of life. And I was troubled about the existence of God. For some time in my childhood the only concrete proof I could find was that people did not have children until they were married: this, I argued, showed clearly that God really did preside over human affairs and took care to send children to couples after marriage. But when I discovered that birth was a biological process that was possible without marriage, I realized at once that the only tangible proof of God's intervention in human affairs had been removed. Night after night, on going to bed, I used to plead with God to send me that night some sign to prove His existence —some dream, some token, however slight, that would indicate that He was there and had heard me. None ever came. This was not the kind of thing I could discuss with my father.

As I grew older, and became interested in Jewish history and the whole fascinating process of the development of Jewish tradition, I accepted Jewish orthodoxy and my father's synthesis out of pride in the Jewish cultural heritage, and was less bothered about the existence of God. I came to see the theological questions as subordinate to the more practical question of the basis of a culture. There was a period in my teens when, passionately devoted to the Zionist cause, I saw myself in a Messianic role leading the Jewish people back to their ancient homeland. And I remember during my first year at Edinburgh University thinking that the summit of my academic ambitions would be to become professor of English at the newly founded Hebrew University in Jerusalem. It is perhaps a sad and certainly an ironic comment on human affairs that when I was offered that position at the end of the war I declined it.

The change which resulted in my life when I left school and entered Edinburgh University was enormous, and had far-reaching consequences. At school I had done my work and gone home, taking no part in sports or other extra-curricular activities. But the university was different. There was a great variety of social and intellectual life outside the lecture room, and it was not mostly confined, as nonacademic school activities were, to Friday night and Saturday; I found myself joining societies, writing for the student magazine, making friends among my non-Jewish fellow students. I discovered, to my delighted astonishment, that my fluency in speech and facility in turning verse, which had helped to amuse the family at home but which I had not till now thought to be in any degree out-of-the-way qualities, made me a popular and sought-after figure at the university, and Lionel, too, found that his oratorical gifts and genius as a raconteur gave him an important place in student life. I remember, after taking part in the annual Associated Societies Debate early in my undergraduate career, I was congratulated by the chairman, who remarked: "I suppose at school you must have run the Literary and Debating Society single handed." I merely smiled in reply: I did not like to tell him that at school I was never able to attend the Literary and Debating Society because it met on Friday nights, nor did I admit that this was my first appearance at a public debate. In due course I became senior president of the English Literature Society, junior president of the Diagnostic Society, and literary editor of *The Student*. I found myself being continually surprised that I was actually taking a prominent part in such activities.

The sense of liberation was intoxicating. I had not realized before how narrow and indeed lonely my life had previously been. There was, of course, the family circle with its loyalties and affections; but in my last years at school, when my literary interests were growing and I was going through a phase of romantic introspection, I had no one to discuss these things with, and got into the habit of going for long walks alone. I even grew for a while apart from Lionel, with whom I had grown up in closest association, for as we became older our interests came to differ. And I had no close friends at school—at least none whom I saw anything of outside school hours. But now I was free of a new and richer world, and not only free of it but sought after by it.

At first this had no effect on my Jewish feeling. I was, in fact, aggressively Jewish, taking every opportunity of pointing out my background and, I am afraid, rather snobbishly insisting on its superiority. When, in my first year at the university, I fell sentimentally in love with a fellow student (it was an extraordinary calf-love affair: I had hardly spoken to a girl except my sisters before that) we exchanged passionate avowals and then decided to part forever because my being Jewish made any further relationship impossible. (The decision, I should add, was mine, not hers. It never occurred to *her* that there was a barrier.) I had a broken heart for almost a year after that. I also did some serious thinking. To my father, it was inconceivable that I should even take a non-Jewish girl out to tea. Indeed, it was inconceivable to him that Lionel or I should take *any* girl, even one of deep Jewish orthodoxy, out to tea or anywhere else. The Daiches boys didn't do that. We were the rabbi's sons, and known, and we were not to be seen going about with a girl. When the time came, we would be introduced to beautiful, intelligent, and perhaps also wealthy Jewish girls from cities which had larger Jewish populations than Edinburgh, and we would then doubtless fall in love and get married. Or, if we did not fall in love with the first one provided, there would be others. Here again, my father's innocence was shattering. He was bitterly angry as well as puzzled when he once met Lionel walking with an extremely respectable Jewish girl in an Edinburgh street. This was when I was having my first romantic love affair with the non-Jewish student, and it occurred to me that if my father felt this way when Lionel went for a walk with a Jewish girl from an orthodox family, what would he have said had he known that every day I had been walking my girl home from the university?

Oddly enough, my father never made any objection to our going to university dances, whatever his private misgivings might have been. But it was unthinkable that we should take a girl to a dance we attended; we went alone, or as a member of a large party where the couples were not paired off. What my father thought we did at these dances I cannot imagine. The difficulty, if not the sheer impossibility, of going to a dance alone never seems to have occurred to him. Lionel, always more enterprising than I was in these matters, once arranged to take to a university dance the daughter of a highly respected member of the Edinburgh Jewish community. When my father found out that he intended to take this girl to the dance, he was thunderstruck. An enormous storm broke, and the upshot was that Lionel went to the dance alone. Fortunately, he went in his capacity as business manager of the university society that was running the dance, so he had an excuse for breezing in by himself, as though to see how things were going.

Deceit was forced on me by degrees. My father knew that I was a member of several university societies attended by both sexes. He knew that girls attended the university lectures. Presumably it was all right if I got into conversation with a girl after a lecture or after a society meeting. Was it all right to walk a few steps while talking with her? If so, how many? The position was, in fact, ludicrous. I began to ask myself whether this "so far and no further" attitude between Jews and non-Jews was healthy or desirable or even, over any length of time, possible. And when I found that I made friends at the university to whom I could talk more freely and satisfyingly than to any Jewish friends or relations, the problem became more acute still. No one had warned me of the possibility that I might find some non-Jews more *sympathique* than any Jews I knew. This was a most disturbing revelation to me, and it made toeing the invisible line imposed by the policy of Jewish self-segregation not only physically almost impossible but a great strain psychologically. It was all very well for my father to speak to enthusiastic gentile audiences at Burns clubs or anti-Hitler protest meetings; he was a rabbi, with his status, his mission, his publicly recognized postion as a Jewish leader. My position was very

[183]

different: I was exploring friendship for the first time in my life, and I found the invisible line increasingly illogical. The first time that I took a girl to a dance was at the end of my first year at the university when, secretly and with every kind of precaution against being found out at home, I took the fellow student I was in love with. (Let the psychologists say what they like about the sense of guilt, but the fact is I had a wonderful time. I was a poor dancer; most of the time we sat in a corner and talked.) The second time was some years later, when I had matured considerably both intellectually and emotionally: I took then another fellow student, who was to become my wife.

Thus it was that a policy of anguished reconsideration of the relation between my Jewish background and my non-Jewish environment was forced on me. It was a long, difficult, and painful process, which was not complete until the end of my years as a research student at Oxford. My deep affection and admiration for my father never altered, but I had a sense of living on the edge of a precipice. I would come home from a walk on the Pentlands with a group of my university friends (or with only one of them), to find, say, preparations for Passover in progress, and I would feel as though I was walking from one century into another. My non-Jewish friends made things as easy for me as they could. They knew I ate no meat at their houses; they knew that Friday night and Saturday were impossible times for me; when I was asked to take part in a play put on by one of the university societies, the performance was arranged for the evenings of Tuesday, Wednesday, and Thursday instead of the usual Thursday, Friday, and Saturday. But though this saved me inconvenience it only increased my sense of living in two worlds, and sometimes in an abyss between them.

[184]

I remember particularly one winter evening coming from a gay meeting of a university society to a Friday night service at the synagogue. There was only a handful of people, old men mostly, at the service, and as the slow and melancholy notes of the concluding hymn, *Yigdal*, rose thinly up to the roof, I thought of the centuries during which this hymn had been sung, of long-dead Jewish congregations in Provence, the Rhineland, and Poland, who had held so steadfastly to their Jewish way of life and passed their heritage unchanged on to their children. I thought of the long roll of Jewish martyrs, those who had given their lives for the "sanctification of the Name." I thought of my own ancestors, of my grandfather and of *his* father, Aryeh Zvi Daiches, whose picture I had seen on the wall of my grandfather's study, a noble-looking man in a fur-trimmed cap, one of the innumerable Jewish scholars and teachers from whom I was descended.

My affection for my father increased, if possible, as I realized how innocent and how vulnerable he was. At the same time, I read Jewish apologetics with an increasingly critical eye. I reread my father's *Aspects of Judaism,* noting in the margin arguments which I could not find convincing. I studied the Jewish prayer book, and noted the difference between the strains of noble piety and crude superstition. I came to see the Hebrew Bible as a fascinating record of the spiritual development of a people rather than as a book of conduct inspired by God. When I went to Oxford, and engaged in research on English translations of the Hebrew Bible, I pursued my Hebrew studies and read more and more about Biblical history and about the development of Judaism. I read much Zionist literature, as well as modern Hebrew poetry. I translated some of the poems of Jehudah Halevi into Scots. Unconsciously, I was preparing for a showdown with my father. Whatever happened, I was not to be accused of lack of knowledge of or affection for my ancestral heritage.

All the time I was at Oxford I was wrestling with the problem of reconciling my deep love for my parents, and my persisting affection for the Jewish traditions with which I was brought up, with the psychological realities of my present situation. Night after night I lay awake conducting imaginary dialogues with my father. I was profoundly in love with my former fellow student at Edinburgh, and though I had never formally proposed we both knew that sooner or later we must and would marry. (And let me at this point give the lie direct to those who claim that intermarriage never works: I write within a month of our eighteenth wedding anniversary, and I know of no marriage which has been as consistently happy and mutually rewarding as ours.) At the same time I was, of my own choice, conducting the services at the somewhat makeshift Jewish synagogue in Oxford, and writing my weekly letters to my father in Hebrew. It was not a happy time, and though of course I remember many individual happy occasions at Oxford it is hardly an exaggeration, though it sounds melodramatic, to say that my years there were blighted by the nightmarish situation in which I found myself.

Showdowns between different generations are never really possible, and I learned that, too, eventually. True, my father was innocent and vulnerable; but he had his own dignity and his own sense of responsibility toward his congregation. There was a point at which argument failed, and he fell back on that dignity and that responsibility. For all our clannishness and profound mutual affection and loyalty, we were not a demonstrative family. Only at the moment of bitterest difference between my father and myself did he bring himsef to voice sentiments of tenderness and of love. Not long afterward, when I was on my way to America with my wife, a radiogram was brought to me as I lay, slightly seasick, on my bunk. It was from my father and mother, and read: "Yom Kippur blessings." It was the Day of Atonement, 1937.

I accepted an academic position in America at the University of Chicago, purely for my father's sake. I went there so that he would not feel embarrased (or even, as he once desperately suggested, compelled to resign his position as rabbi in Edinburgh) by anything that I had done or would do. I had at that time no particular interest in America, nor was I at all anxious to go there: I resigned my fellowship at Balliol with reluctance. Yet of course there was the sense of high adventure and, more important, the knowledge that I was sharing that adventure, that my wife and I were starting out for the new world together. Once there, we had an orthodox Jewish marriage for my father's sake, and looked forward to returning permanently to Britain after a few years. As it happened, though we came home for a visit in 1939, the war kept us in America for many years more. They were in many respects happy and fruitful years, and we made firm friends there. But we felt ourselves, particularly during the war, to be exiles, cut off from the country and the people that claimed our deepest attachment. I was horrified when one of my former teachers at Edinburgh wrote to me in America applauding my decision to "get out while the going was good." I pestered the British consular authorities in Chicago for advice on how to get back, and, when a scheme was introduced facilitating the voluntary return of British subjects residing abroad provided they would join one of the services on arrival, I signed up at once, stipulating only that my wife and two children should be given transportation back with me, for otherwise I would be unable to support them. While waiting for transportation I was given a position with British Information Services in New York, and after a while I was requisitioned by the British Embassy in Washington, where I remained (except for two official visits back to England) until 1946. By that time I had long since lost my place in the academic queue in England, and was glad to accept an attractive offer from Cornell, where we remained for five years before a suitable academic opening in England made our permanent return possible. My American friends will think this an ungenerous and perhaps even an inaccurate account of my feelings toward my long American sojourn. They know how easily and happily my wife and I fitted into the American academic community where I worked. Yet always we talked and planned of coming home. We lived on two levels, as it were, the immediate present, busily and happily in America, and the deeper nostalgic level, which we revealed only to each other.

If I were writing a novel based on my own life it would end with the summer of 1939, when my wife and I, with our small son, came home to the happy ending that I had always profoundly believed in. We took a cottage in Perthshire by the River Tay for the summer months, while I did some writing. My father and mother made inquiries and found a nearby farmhouse to let for August, so they spent August there, just across the river from us. Part of that time my wife's people were with us too (and how tactful and understanding they had been throughout the whole affair!). We would go over to the farmhouse on Friday night, for the traditional Sabbath eve dinner. Somehow an inclusive world had been established, which took us all in. Arguments, I knew now, were futile and cruel. I remember a sunny afternoon in the garden of our cottage, with my parents leaning over their grandson in his pram. It was about ten days before the beginning of World War II.

The last scene of all was in December, 1944. I was working in the British Embassy in Washington, and had been flown over to Britain to spend some time at the Ministry of Information in London. I managed to get a week's leave in Edinburgh. I had not seen my parents since that summer of 1939, a time that now seemed worlds away. As the taxi stopped outside the familiar house—shabbier than I remembered it, but otherwise startlingly the same—I found it hard to believe that this was me, returning, in 1944. The front door was open, and I went in, and there in the drawing room, huddled over a small electric heater, were my father and mother. It was a bitterly cold day, and coal was in short supply. My father had his arm in a cast; he was recovering from the accident I mentioned earlier. I sat between him and Mother, and we talked.

My father's arm mended steadily, and the following Saturday he insisted (against all advice) on going to shul and preaching. I went with him, holding his arm so that he would not slip on the icy pavement. He looked frail and worn as he stood in the pulpit to begin his sermon, but his voice was as strong as ever. His tallith kept slipping off his shoulders, and, since he had only the use of one arm, he was unable to put it back: I had to go up and help him. He took as his text the account (from that day's portion of the Law) of Jacob sending young Joseph to seek his brothers in Shechem, and went on to discuss the whole question of youth going out beyond the ken of the older generation.

[189]

Why should Jacob have allowed his beloved young son to go out into the dangers which he knew were awaiting him? Was not this being a bad father? No; Jacob was right. There is a point beyond which a parent cannot be protective toward his children, and Jewish parents often err through not realizing this. Jacob was right in sending his rather pampered young son into dangers away from home: Joseph would have to work out his own salvation. And perhaps the older generation can learn from the younger. I think he was speaking to me, offering full understanding and reconciliation. But, as always, he was more at home in public than in private utterance. A handful of regular attenders, a few American Jewish soldiers, a couple of R.A.F. boys on leave, heard my father's last testament: but he and I knew whom it was meant for.

I left Edinburgh the next day: "It won't be five years before I am back again to see you next time," I said to my father on departing. But I never saw him again. Though I did not know it at the time, he was in fact dying of a disease he had long concealed from everybody. If he had gone into a hospital for appropriate treatment in time, he could have been cured easily. But he hated the idea of a deputy doing his work; this was his congregation, he had welded it together, and he would minister to it until the end. And he did. After his accident he continued to preach regularly, attend meetings, deliver public speeches, and carry on all his multifarious duties as rabbi, until, some five months later, he collapsed one evening after a day crowded with meetings and died shortly afterward.

None of his children was with him when he died. Lionel was in the army in Italy; Sylvia was on a war job in London; Beryl was on war service with the W.A.A.F.; I was in Washington. Only my mother sat by his bedside at the end. "If only I had five more years," he said to her when he realized he was dying, "there is still so much to do." He repeated, literally with his very last breath, the profession that a dying Jew traditionally makes of his faith: *"Adonai hu Ha-Elohim"* (the Lord is God).

I received the cable announcing his death before the arrival of the letters telling me of his illness. And a week afterward I received a letter from my father himself (transatlantic mails could be very slow in wartime); it had been written a few days before his final collapse. He spoke cheerfully of his regaining use of his "strong right arm," and congratulated me on my promotion to a more responsible position at the embassy. Months later, when I was in Edinburgh again, I was told by a member of my father's congregation who had visited him two days before his death that one of the first things my father had said to him was: "David has got a fine new position at the British Embassy in Washington."

Many times since his death people have suggested to me that I should write something about my father, or edit his sermons, or collect his essays and letters. But his sermons and his essays and his letters are not important in themselves: it was his personality that gave him life. He was a great preacher, but not a great sermon writer: his life was greater than his works. Indeed, his life *was* his work, and to separate the two is to do both an injustice. It is not my father's philosophy, his dialectical skill or his religious thought that was remarkable. His letters to the *Scotsman* divorced from the context of the particular occasions that prompted them have no especial interest today. These things are part of his biography, and must not be separated from it. But again, the mere facts of my father's life are

[191]

of no importance. In any case I know only a few of them. I do know my own life, however, and in telling part of that story I can tell all I know about my father. Once, asked whether he believed in personal immortality (a question on which I do not believe he ever committed himself), he smiled and said that one lives most effectively after death in the memories of those whom one has loved and taught. He was right: these chapters from my autobiography turn out to be a tribute to him. He is the hero, not I. And if this means that the story is a tragedy, he would not have flinched from that. The tragic hero, said Aristotle, has his *hamartia*, his flaw, but he is also a person of some stature and nobility.

Yet the story is tragic only if we read it too literally. True, my father's synthesis, however brilliantly illustrated in his own life, proved incapable of transmission to his children, at least in the form he gave it. His ultimate recognition of this was perhaps rueful rather than either complacent or tragic. But he went on with his ministry to the end, pursuing his chosen way of life with heroic dignity. The last thing he wrote was a series of charming essays for young people on the Jewish festivals. Perhaps, in Talmudic phrase, his works exceeded his wisdom; his life is more memorable than his writings. And Rabbi Eleazar the son of Azaryah said that he whose wisdom exceeds his works is like a tree with many branches and few roots, easily overturned by the wind, while he whose works exceed his wisdom is like a tree with few branches and many roots, which cannot be overturned by all the winds that blow.